Welfare and
the Constitution

Sotirios A. Barber

PRINCETON UNIVERSITY PRESS

PRINCETON AND OXFORD

Library of Congress Cataloging-in-Publication Data

Barber, Sotirios A.
Welfare and the Constitution / Sotirios A. Barber.
p. cm.
Includes bibliographical references and index.
ISBN: 0-691-11448-X (alk. paper)
1. Constitutional law—United States—Philosophy.
2. Welfare state—United States—Philosophy. I. Title.

KF4552 .B368 2003
342.73'02—dc21   2002193000

British Library Cataloging-in-Publication Data is available

This book has been composed in Palatino Typeface

Printed on acid-free paper. ∞
www.pupress.princeton.edu

Printed in the United States of America
1 3 5 7 9 10 8 6 4 2

For Alex and Leah

CONTENTS

ACKNOWLEDGMENTS

My THANKS to the American Council of Learned Societies and to Notre Dame's College of Arts and Letters for supporting a sabbatical year devoted to this project. I'm grateful also to the participants of several symposia and conferences at which I presented portions of my argument over the last several years, especially Jack Balkin, Christopher Eisgruber, Mark Graeber, Sanford Levinson, Stephen Macedo, Linda McClain, Frank Michelman, Lawrence Sager, Jeffrey Tulis, and Mark Tushnet. I am grateful also to Gerard Bradley, Karen Flax, James Fleming, Robert George, and Walter Murphy for their comments on drafts of the manuscript. My thanks, finally, to Denise Baikie for work above and beyond the call in preparing the manuscript for publication. This would have been a better book had time permitted more of my attention to the advice and criticism of these individuals.

THIS BOOK is about the general welfare and the American Constitution. Its central question is whether government in America is constitutionally obligated to do what it reasonably can to secure a good life for all its people. This question is a complex of issues in constitutional theory and moral philosophy. It implicates secondary philosophic issues of moral metaphysics and epistemology (Is the general welfare an objective state of affairs? Can we approximate knowledge of it?). It involves the primary moral question of what the general welfare is. It implicates questions of political philosophy and the social sciences concerning what approximation of the general welfare is reasonably within the nation's aspirations. It embraces questions of constitutional history and theory running from the normative logic of the American founding (Did the framers design a charter of negative liberties or a charter of positive benefits?) to the success of "checks and balances" as a method of constitutional maintenance. And it embraces questions of legal doctrine like the national government's authority under the general welfare clause of Article I and the respective powers in this area of legislatures and courts and the national government and the states.

Readers can appreciate the complexities of the subject and still wonder whether the central question is worth much of their time. Some readers will quickly agree that our governments have some obligation to work for the general welfare, whatever the general welfare might be. Salaried agent-representatives of the people have at least a moral obligation to try to keep the promises they make to the electorate, and people typically vote and pay taxes voluntarily only for benefits promised or received. Informed readers will connect this moral obligation to the Constitution because they know that moral outlook influences constitutional interpretation and that parts of the Constitution, like the Preamble, the general welfare clause, and the equal protection clause, can be read to constitutionalize some obligation to pursue some understanding of the general welfare.

For these reasons some readers will doubt that honest and competent observers could declare that government in America has no constitutional duty to work for the good of the people it governs. These readers do not have to be persuaded to the central thesis of this book: that the issue is not whether government should promote welfare but whose welfare government should promote and why the welfare of some but not others. These readers might well ask why government should fund judicial and executive processes for the collection of private debt yet decline to fund child care for the working poor. They might ask why the state should employ conscription in wartime and the criminal law in peacetime to deprive some persons of their youthful wherewithal (their property in a state of nature) and not take money from the monied for common schools.

Though *some* positive governmental duty thus seems hard to deny, a doctrine of no unqualified constitutional duty to benefit anyone (or something close to it) has been proposed, and by voices prestigious and powerful. Many academic lawyers and federal judges hold that no government in America has an unconditional federal constitutional duty to provide any substantive benefit to anyone—no constitutional duty to provide police protection, for example, even to a child of four against the reasonably predictable, because repeated, violence of a disturbed parent. In 1989, this troubling proposition became the official position of the U.S. Supreme Court.

The mere fact that important officials hold a position may not justify the exertion needed to refute it, for no one is above the occasional statement that condemns itself, and political opposition to such statements need not be accompanied by extensive scholarly analysis. But the doctrine of no unconditional constitutional duty to benefit the people in any way, though alarming and false, is not beneath the effort to refute. The doctrine can be explained not as chilling indifference to the people's welfare but as thoughtful opposition to the so-called welfare state. The lawyers and judges who espouse the doctrine seem to feel that finding government constitutionally obligated to secure the physical safety of its people makes it harder to deny what they seem committed to deny: that government is constitutionally obligated to combat poverty with benefits like food stamps and monthly welfare checks.

The Constitution is a self-declared law, and a constitutional duty would generally be considered a legal duty. The prospect of any legal duty to help the poor as such is unacceptable to many people, including some who say they think it morally imperative to help the deserving poor through private charity. They oppose state provision for the poor for reasons ranging from a love of selected liberties and a selective hostility to "redistributive government" (as if there were some other kind of government) to a belief that state provision for the poor exacerbates problems it would solve. Some critics of "welfare" hold that in a large country whose civic culture respects personal privacy, gives private persons rather than government the benefit of the doubt, and relies mostly on the impersonal processes of courts and bureaucracies to redeem entitlements and enforce rights, a general legal right not to starve would inevitably mean aid for some who neither need aid nor deserve it. Critics of the dole typically add that the welfare claims of able-bodied individuals who avoid work and bear children beyond their means are ultimately claims against taxpayers. And taxpayers are often outraged by what they believe to be the large number of self-indulgent, dishonest, and even arrogant persons (arrogant because "rights" are involved) "on welfare."

Proposing that help for the poor can be a mandate of the Constitution—as if statutory entitlements were not sufficient—might make "welfare" even more offensive to its critics. In nations that use courts to enforce rights against majoritarian government, constitutionalizing support for the poor can compound the anger of taxpayers with populist resentment of unelected judges intruding on democratic choice. As these sentiments have combined in some quarters, hostility toward the welfare state has swelled to threaten the idea of government established and ordained to secure the well-being of all.

Under ideal conditions, like jobs for the able and adequate charity for the disabled, a principle of "no duty to benefit" thus may enhance democracy (by disabling courts) and the prospects of virtue over vice (by combating dependency)—results that are presumed to benefit everyone. To supplement this appeal to goods like democracy and self-reliance, critics of aid to the poor add arguments from history and moral theory. These arguments include an account of the framers of the Constitution as free marketeers, not social democrats; an argument that the welfare state tries to coerce people into conforming to, or paying for, arbitrary conceptions of the good life; and arguments that the "general welfare" is nothing more than an aggregate of the subjective preferences of individuals and thus whatever allocation of goods results from the self-interested calculations of individuals in either the free market or the open and unobstructed electoral processes of majoritarian democracy. No unconditional constitutional duty to do anything good for anyone can thus seem a politically responsible idea—that is, one thought to serve the general welfare. The no-duty-to-benefit thesis deserves refutation for this reason.

Although this book rejects all constitutional arguments against aid for the poor as largely either false, misleading, or self-defeating, it defends the so-called welfare state in ways that give the other side its limited due. The book agrees especially with one assumption of the other side: There is indeed a connection between police protection and aid for the poor such that you may not in fairness support one without supporting the other. Police protection turns out to be a form of (redistributive) welfare; protect people from violence and you must in justice show why it is not in their welfare to protect them from poverty and ignorance. Critics of the welfare state deserve credit for this insight even though it works against them. Though I also agree with the other side that the general welfare and the "welfare state" (the state of poor support) are conceptually distinct and, under some circumstances and in some respects, even opposed, I'll argue that the general welfare remains a constitutional aspiration that must include the welfare of the poor and that cannot be conceived solely in terms of market allocations or electoral outcomes. I'll argue further that there is constitutional power and a corresponding duty to pursue this constitutional aspiration, even if one doubts, as I do, that the Constitution is adequate to its ends.

In this book, I urge constitutional theorists to reconsider:

- False assumptions regarding the Constitution's general normative nature. Present assumptions give pride of constitutional place to institutional (process) norms and negative rights. Sounder assumptions would elevate constitutional *powers* and *ends* over institutional principles and negative liberties.
- False assumptions about the constitutional text: that it guarantees no positive benefits; that its framers would have *listed* such benefits had they intended them; that the task of progressive scholarship is *either* to construe an antiwelfarist constitution in light of philosophic principles from "beyond its four corners" (theories of justice, "basic needs," "social citizenship," "human flourishing," etc.) *or* to derive the missing welfare rights from constitutional institutions and negative liberties (a right to education as prerequisite to democratic citizenship, for example, or as resulting from a right to equal respect and concern).
- False assumptions about the scope of state-facilitated welfare—that "welfare" comprehends "poor support" and help for the aged and the disabled, not all that the state does for its people.
- False assumptions about the nature of governmental action: that there are relevant distinctions between state action and inaction (widely held in the polity despite wide rejection in the academy) and especially between regulatory and redistributive policies (still falsely assumed by many academics).

This book brings contrary assumptions to bear on the welfare problem. I try to show that the Constitution is, always was, and in a sense had to be a welfarist constitution—one that subordinates institutions and negative liberties to constitutional *powers* and *ends*, entities that imply each other. I contend that the question never really was *whether* welfare, but what welfare, welfare for whom, and why for some and not all. I contend further that there is no successful way to deny a fully constitutional obligation (not just a moral or prudential obligation) to facilitate the well-being of all responsible persons. And I argue that this obligation is in every way *foundational* to the very institutions and negative rights that are widely but erroneously held to limit the pursuit of constitutional ends.

This book proposes that: (1) James Madison and others in the early tradition were right to view the Constitution as a means to desirable ends. They were right to treat the people's well-being as more important than any institutional form. They were right not because they occupied an original position but because their ends-oriented view of American constitutions is the only way to make sense of the nation's constitutional experience. (2) No argument of any sort—historical, scientific, metaethical, ethical, or prudential—defeats an ends-oriented or "welfarist" or "benefits" understanding of the Constitution. (3) Constitutional scholars who respect a liberal order can and should debate substantive theories of the general welfare and use those theories to evaluate public policies in the Constitution's name.

I propose, as a working hypothesis with which the needed discussion might begin, a theory drawn in large part from traditional sources like *The Federalist*. This theory is fully consistent with constitutionalist principles. It respects the claims of (constitution-minded) taxpayers and legislators, admitting only a secondary role for judges. It respects Lockean values like work, property, and personal responsibility. And it shows how opponents of state help for the poor often disappoint their own principles.

The book concludes with a chapter that is submitted as a prolegomenon to questions beyond the limited ambitions of American constitutional theory as the theory of an instrumental constitution. One such question is what political actors, like judges, should do to advance constitutional ends in fact-specific concrete cases. Constitutional theory cannot answer such questions. But constitutional theory can show, as I try to show, how the Constitution can influence or bias decision makers in different categories of cases. Another question beyond constitutional theory is whether the actual, working constitutional system is adequate to its chief end, the welfare of its people. I can say whether the Constitution is adequate to the people's welfare—but only as a formal matter of legal competence or power, not as a matter of empirical constitutional culture, though I do offer an opinion about the latter. Having begun the book by making the most of Michael Walzer's proposal that every state is a welfare state and that "welfare" embraces all that a state does to benefit its people, I end by suggesting that the welfare debate involves the well-being of all Americans, individually and collectively, not just the young, the disabled, and the poor.

Welfare and the Constitution

Chapter One

INTRODUCTION: EVERY STATE

A WELFARE STATE

THIS BOOK examines the constitutional dimensions of the welfare debate in America. The precise shape of state-facilitated welfare here and elsewhere will depend on results of policy experiments either under way or anticipated and on the contest among philosophic frameworks for describing those results. Because I share to some limited extent the conventional view that constitutional questions differ from policy questions, this book proposes few specific policies in the Constitution's name. But I shall emphasize here what I have argued elsewhere: the American Constitution makes sense (and originally made sense) only in light of general substantive ends like national security, freedom of conscience, domestic tranquility, and the people's economic well-being. For this reason, fidelity to the American Constitution entails a concern for more than negative constitutional rights, constitutional procedures, and institutional forms; it also entails a concern for what James Madison called "the solid happiness of the people." And this must be the chief concern—the end to which all other concerns must bend. As Madison reminded critics who saw the ratification debate as a contest between confederated and unitary or "consolidated" forms of government, the American Revolution teaches that "the real welfare of the great body of the people is the supreme object to be pursued; and . . . no form of Government whatever, has any other value, than as it may be fitted for the attainment of this object."[1]

I try here to defend Madison's statement about the end of government and to show what it imports for the basic normative nature of the American Constitution, for the cultivation and maintenance of a people that appreciates such a constitution as its own, and for constitutional theory as a field of academic inquiry. I try to persuade constitutional theorists to take the Constitution's Preamble seriously and turn to the hard philosophic and scientific work of formulating a forthrightly substantive theory of "the general Welfare." I contend against

---

[1] Jacob E. Cooke, ed., *The Federalist* (Middletown, Conn.: Wesleyan University Press, 1961), No. 45, p. 309. Subsequent references to *The Federalist* will take the following form: (paper number: page number of Cooke's edition).

scholars who argue on multiple philosophic grounds against the possibility of such a theory. I show that the Constitution itself presupposes such a theory and implies guidelines for developing it. I derive these guidelines from the constitutional text and then use them to formulate a working theory of the general welfare, which theory I submit to the debate about the substance of the nation's values and character. According to this working theory, the Constitution not only permits but under some social conditions can even require such benefits as Social Security pensions for the aged and disabled, Medicaid for the poor, the late Aid to Families with Dependent Children (AFDC), and, above all, a liberal or self-critically secular education at public expense for the children of all who want it.

I also argue that because enforcing many such state duties falls more to the taxpaying electorate than to the judiciary, declining public sympathy for the poor (and other developments, like religious-based hostility to the public schools as fonts of secular reasonableness) indicates that the authors of *The Federalist* erred in thinking they could maintain the Constitution by relying mostly, if not exclusively, on what they called "the private interest of every individual" to be "a centinel over the public rights" (51:349). They erred in thinking they could avoid active governmental efforts to foster a citizenry whose members were at once personally responsible and public-spirited. By book's end I hope to persuade the reader that the debate over welfare for the poor is really a debate about constitutional and even cultural reform, a debate about the meaning of "responsibility" and the character and true well-being not just of the poor but of the nation as a cultural whole.

Following my discussion later in this introductory chapter about matters of terminology and argumentative strategy, my first step is to describe the basic normative properties of the American Constitution as a legal document. I contend in chapter 2 that the Constitution is more a charter of positive benefits—a positive or welfarist constitution, if you will—than a charter of negative liberties and that a central question for constitutional theory is not *whether* state-facilitated welfare but *what* state-facilitated welfare and *for whom*. Answering this question involves issues with philosophic and scientific dimensions, like the best conceptions of personal and national well-being both in theory and reasonably within the nation's aspirations. This book would persuade constitutional theorists to do what they can to help answer this complex of questions and to publicize its importance for the social sciences and the humanities generally. But no such commitment of resources is likely where constitutional theorists are either persuaded or simply assume that constitutional guarantees are limited by and large to what courts can enforce and thus to the definition of citizenship and participatory rights, the horizontal and vertical arrangements of governmental offices and powers, procedural protections for persons accused of crime, the right to equal concern and respect for some minorities, and a handful of substantive rights understood as "negative liberties" or qualified exemptions from governmental power.

This list of the Constitution's normative functions is conventional wisdom among today's constitutional theorists. The list was less modest in times past. Today's view of constitutional functions not only fails to reflect the constitutionalism of the Progressive Era and the New Deal; it fails also to comprehend Jefferson's proposition, asserted to be "self-evident" in the Declaration of Independence, that legitimate governments are established by people "to effect their Safety and Happiness." The current view falls short of Madison's commitment to the people's welfare because promoting the people's welfare entails affirmative governmental duties and corresponding rights. The current view excludes any right in the people to what Lincoln called a "government whose leading object is to elevate the condition of men."[2] Far short of grand ends like the people's welfare and happiness, the current view excludes even a constitutional right to police protection against third-party or "private" violence, and this notwithstanding the Constitution's situation in a philosophic tradition that puts protection from private violence "at the heart of the social contract."[3] The dominant view at present is that affirmative rights—even to police protection—are alien both to the constitutional text and to a constitutional tradition dominated by free-market ideology. Talk of affirmative substantive rights is supposed to undermine negative rights like the freedoms of speech and religion and blur the distinction between totalitarian and free-world constitutions. And the question of "what welfare and for whom" is supposed to confront insuperable metaphysical and epistemological objections to any hope for objective answers. In chapters 2 through 4, I try to meet these historical, philosophic, and policy objections to the positive turn that this book proposes for constitutional theory.

Chapters 2 through 4 do work that is largely negative; they criticize conventional thinking in hopes of reversing the present presumption against a welfarist view of the Constitution. Chapter 5 is the positive heart of the book; it sets forth a substantive theory of the general wel-

[2] Abraham Lincoln, "Message to Congress: July 4, 1861," in Roy P. Basler, ed., *Abraham Lincoln: His Speeches and Writings* (New York: Grosset and Dunlap, 1946), 607.

[3] See Robin West, "Rights, Capabilities and the Good Society," *Fordham Law Review* 69 (2001): 1908–9, 1922–23; see also Steven J. Heyman, "The First Duty of Government: Protection, Liberty and the Fourteenth Amendment," *Duke Law Journal* 41 (1991): 508, 530–45.

fare and submits it to constitutional theory as a field of academic inquiry that should be open to such submissions. In keeping with my understanding of the general welfare—its nature and the normative gap between (presumably) real goods like the general welfare and our theories of these goods—I submit my theory as a working hypothesis for the substantive debate about the nation's values, a debate to which constitutional theorists can make special contributions. Chapter 5 begins by sketching some formal principles of the Constitution as a charter of positive benefits; the aim is to show how these formal principles can influence theories of the people's well-being, the corresponding duties of officials, and the power of constitutional government to shape the attitudes of its people. The chapter then sketches what can be described as a theory of the general welfare that is social-democratic in substance yet largely "conservative" or at least "traditional" in derivation and "perfectionist" in execution. Deploying arguments from my previous works, present-day progressive writers, neo-Aristotelians, and American classics like *The Federalist* and the speeches of Lincoln, the chapter proposes that the Constitution promises a government that is actively concerned with substantive goods like children who are healthy and educated to think for themselves on the basis of evidence available in principle to humankind in general, as opposed to this or that religious, sexual, or racial perspective. The chapter also proposes that constitutional government in America can legitimately foster personal responsibility, and that for the same reason that it can foster personal responsibility it can legitimately discourage racism, forms of religious zeal, and a self-indulgence that breed indifference and blindness to public purposes, hostility to the ends of a liberal regime, and an incapacity to act on reasons that anonymous, competent, and autonomous persons can recognize as good reasons.

The book's final chapter exposes my pessimism about the shape of things to come in America and reflects my belief that the Constitution is imperfect, even by its own standards. Fidelity to the Constitution hardly precludes this belief,[4] for the ratification provisions of Article VII and the amending provisions of Article V combine to imply at least the possibility of constitutional inadequacy. We are thus entitled to ask whether the government established to promote the general welfare can do much to redeem that promise. This question is largely beyond the scope of this book. Whether and under what conditions the nation's public philosophy is ever likely to shift in a positive direction are questions *for* constitutional theory but not *of* constitutional theory;

[4] See J. M. Balkin, "Agreements with Hell and Other Objects of Our Faith," *Fordham Law Review* 65 (1997): 1703–38.

they can be answered, if at all, only by the social sciences. Whether the national government has the requisite competence as a matter of current legal doctrine is also a question *for* but not *of* constitutional theory, for the focus of constitutional theory, I have contended elsewhere and assume here, should be the *Constitution*, not the opinions of some fallible body of interpreters. For these reasons my contribution to the question of constitutional adequacy is mostly a prolegomenon to the question, or to the formal part of the question. I find the pivotal issue to be that which divided Hamilton and Madison over the meaning of the general welfare clause of Article I: how Congress's power to tax and spend for the general welfare is related to the substantive powers (over commerce, the military, etc.) enumerated in Article I, section 8. I show how the principles of the Constitution as a charter of benefits should influence the outcome of that debate. I also address a question that I show to be one of less importance: how the charter of benefits should influence the judicial definition of "welfare rights" under the Fourteenth Amendment.

In the rest of this introductory chapter I describe the general view of the Constitution against which this book contends. I also take up matters of terminology and strategy that bear heavily on my views regarding what well-being in America consists in and the state's duty to promote it.

The Negative-Liberties Model of the Constitution

Present-day students of the Constitution seem generally to assume that, for better or worse, the Constitution leaves government's provision of goods and services, from national defense to pensions and schools, to the play of pluralist political forces represented by elected officials whose decisions are legally restricted solely by judicially declared fundamental rights and structural principles. Thus conceived, the Constitution is a "charter of negative liberties": it guarantees exemptions *from* governmental action, not rights *to* governmental benefits. It imposes no unconditional *duty* to provide, and therefore it guarantees no *right* to any substantive benefit beyond access to the system of interest representation.[5] Whether the Constitution *permits* a specific benefit is held to depend on whether the appropriate level of govern-

---

[5] See, e.g., *Jackson v. City of Joliet*, 715 F. 2d 1200 (7th Cir. 1983); *DeShaney v. Winnebago*, 489 U.S. 189 (1989); David P. Currie, "Positive and Negative Constitutional Rights," *University of Chicago Law Review* 53 (1986): 864, at 864–67; Terrance Sandalow, "Social Justice and Fundamental Law," *Northwestern University Law Review* 88 (1993): 461, at 464–65.

ment (federal or state) delivers the benefit in a legally authorized way and whether the delivery affects rights the judiciary is obligated to pro-tect, like the claimed liberty of business to contract for labor at what-ever price workers will accept or the claimed right of just compensa-tion at public expense when land-use regulations diminish the market value of real estate.

This negative-liberties model of the Constitution organizes much of the debate regarding state-facilitated welfare in America. It excludes any proposal that constitutional theorists find a workable theory of the general welfare as an end that government is constitutionally obligated to pursue. Not that the negative-liberties model is *the* obstacle to what this book proposes; I doubt that constitutional theory generally has much beyond a limited influence on political practice. The negative-liberties model itself may be little more than emblematic of broader cultural forces that constitute the real obstacle to what is here pro-posed. These forces are strong enough to sustain the negative-liberties model in academic venues despite what will quickly prove to be its indefensible, if not fraudulent, character. These same forces also weaken the capacity of jurists, politicians, and ordinary citizens to see the Constitution for what it expressly (in the Preamble) claims to be: an instrument of goods like "the general Welfare." They therefore di-minish hopes that a morally and descriptively truer model will have much of a political impact. Still, if there is a better model, it deserves explication and defense; truth attracts whether it will out politically or not. In addition, it should be hard for American constitutionalists, of all people, to concede that better ideas will probably have utterly no political consequences, and it should be no easier for academics to con-cede that superior theories have little hope in the academy. Also, as we shall see, the cultural forces arrayed against a better model may themselves be influenced by the Constitution, and the very power of these cultural forces undermines a family of (false) arguments against a better model: that constitutionalizing the least deniable of govern-mental benefits (like police protection) puts us on a slippery slope to totalitarian socialism.

While the role of the negative-liberties model in arguments against welfare provision is evident enough, the model gets implicit tribute even from most constitutional arguments *for* state-facilitated welfare. Constitutional arguments for state-facilitated welfare can be classified broadly as either welfare-as-derivative or welfare-as-fundamental, with the derivative view being the most popular by far. The derivative view defends rights to subsistence, employment, education, and the like as the contingent demands of a right to equal concern and respect and the prerequisites to the meaningful exercise of rights like speech and voting and thus to democratic citizenship generally.[6] These arguments for welfare parallel arguments that the welfare state functions as an adjunct of the market by maintaining the market, enabling participation in it, and compensating for its failures.[7] These arguments suggest the negative-liberties model. By treating welfare rights as mere derivatives of structures and exemptions from power, they suggest that exemptions and structures enjoy primacy over constitutional benefits or substantive ends. These arguments do not suggest, as other arguments do,[8] and as I shall press here to the fullest extent, that substantive benefits far beyond police protection are ends to be numbered among a constitutional government's first responsibilities.

Yet arguments for welfare rights as derivative rights remain persuasive and, for some purposes, unavoidable. I resort to a derivative strategy myself when I offer a substantive theory of the general welfare that meets what chapter 5 shows to be a two-part constitutional test of simple ethical attractiveness and cultural appropriateness—an American version of the general welfare that can claim with some plausibility to be more than merely American. But I employ a different strategy when explicating the Constitution's basic normative nature. I explain why in the next section, and in the process I clarify the aims of this

---

[6] See, e.g., Akhil Reed Amar, "Forty Acres and a Mule: A Republican Theory of Minimal Entitlements," *Harvard Journal of Law and Public Policy* 13 (1989): 42–43. See also Frank I. Michelman, "Welfare Rights in a Constitutional Democracy," *Washington University Law Quarterly* (1979): 674–79; Peter B. Edelman, "The Next Century of Our Constitution: Rethinking Our Duty to the Poor," *Hastings Law Journal* 39 (1987): 1, 19–23; Kenneth L. Karst, "Foreword: Equal Citizenship under the Fourteenth Amendment," *Harvard Law Review* 91 (1977): 1, 62; Mark A. Graber, "The Clintonification of American Law: Abortion, Welfare, and Constitutional Theory," *Ohio State Law Journal* 58 (1997): 731, 747, 753–54 (but cf. writers cited with approval at 752).

[7] See, e.g., Robert E. Goodin, "Reasons for Welfare: Economic, Sociological and Political—but Ultimately Moral," in J. Donald Moon, ed., *Responsibility, Rights and Welfare: The Theory of the Welfare State* (Boulder, Colo.: Westview Press, 1988), 29–38.

[8] See, e.g., Susan Bandes, "The Negative Constitution: A Critique," *Michigan Law Review* 88 (1990): 2344–47; Charles L. Black Jr., "Further Reflections on the Constitutional Justice of Livelihood," *Columbia Law Review* (1986): 1105–7, 1113–14; Stephen Holmes, *Passions and Constraint: On the Theory of Liberal Democracy* (Chicago: University of Chicago Press, 1995), chap. 8; Stephen Holmes and Cass R. Sunstein, *The Cost of Rights* (New York: Norton, 1999) 87–94; Frank I. Michelman, "Foreword: On Protecting the Poor through the Fourteenth Amendment," *Harvard Law Review* 83 (1969): 9, 13–15; Lawrence G. Sager, "Justice in Plain Clothes: Reflections on the Thinness of Constitutional Law," *Northwestern University Law Review* 88 (1993): 411–15; Cass R. Sunstein, *The Partial Constitution* (Cambridge: Harvard University Press, 1993), 69–71; Charles A. Reich, "The New Property," *Yale Law Journal* 73 (1964): 733, 786–87; Heyman, "The First Duty of Government," 507; Robert P. George, "Justice, Legitimacy, and Allegiance," in Sotirios A. Barber and Robert P. George, eds., *Constitutional Politics: Essays on Constitution Making, Maintenance, and Change* (Princeton, N.J.: Princeton University Press, 2001), 321.

book, preview some of its main arguments, and defend the use of "welfare provision" and related terms to embrace all that government might do to promote the well-being of its people.

Every State a Welfare State?

In an oft-quoted statement Michael Walzer once proposed that the fundamental duty of any government is to benefit its people. Because every political community claims to provide "for the needs of its members," said Walzer, "every political community is in principle a 'welfare state.'" By the "welfare" for which the state provides, Walzer referred to all state provisions both for the general public and for particular segments of the population; these provisions include but range far beyond benefits designed for the poor.[9]

While not necessarily disagreeing with Walzer's point, most writers apply the term "welfare state" solely to a restricted set of policies and institutions for correcting failures of the market to supply broadly needed goods and, principally, according to Robert Goodin, to safeguard preconditions of the market. Examples of state provision corrective of market failure are mandatory state plans for health insurance and old-age pensions that would fail if the healthy, the young, and the affluent were free to opt out for private plans. Preconditions of the market might include an educated workforce and actors whose relative economic independence of each other (if not the state) enables them to buy and sell at prices that preserve some sense that they are doing what they want to do, not what they have to do, as where the law prohibits involuntary servitude and where an AFDC check, a Medicaid payment, or a public-works job might free a person from acquiescing in the employment offer of a local sweatshop or a neighborhood pimp.[10]

This restrictive sense of "welfare" and "welfare state" has an advantage for defenders of state provision for the poor. When he argues for "welfare" on the ground that it can help to maintain the market, Goodin implies the normative priority of the market. This puts him on common ground with "advocates of the market" from which he can show "that their own principles go a long way toward committing them to at least a minimalist welfare state," leaving "marketeers willing to resist the argument for the welfare state . . . with utterly unpalatable op-

---

[9] Michael Walzer, *Spheres of Justice* (New York: Basic Books, 1983), 68, 64–69.
[10] J. Donald Moon, "Introduction: Responsibility, Rights, and Welfare," in Moon, *Responsibility, Rights, and Welfare*, 2–3; Goodin, "Reasons for Welfare," 24, 27–28, 29–38.

tions at every turn" (42–43). Goodin himself holds that some reasons for the welfare state are "entirely outside" market principles. An example is the respect for human dignity that he says constitutes "[t]he only reason" to respect the free choices that "the market ethos commands." But Goodin doubts that nonmarket principles alone can justify the welfare state, and he offers his market-based argument as supplementary to nonmarket arguments (31, 42).

Market- and citizenship-based arguments for welfare provision treat certain levels of well-being as preconditions of participation in the polity or the market and the provision of corresponding benefits as derivative duties of government. These arguments differ from pure welfarist arguments, those that treat the general welfare as a fundamental obligation of government. Welfarist and nonwelfarist arguments can supplement each other when justifying specific benefits deemed necessary both for human functioning and for productive membership in market or democratic societies.[11] But their differences make these strategies competitive for theoretical and long-range practical purposes. As I shall show in the course of this book, these differences imply different conceptions of citizen virtue (responsibility for self only versus responsibility also for and to others); the state's relationship to the market (as either superior or subordinate); different theories of institutional responsibilities (one favoring legislatures, the other favoring courts); and different theories of constitutional maintenance (one emphasizing education for public-spirited citizenship, the other relying chiefly on "checks and balances").

If, as Walzer says, every political community claims to provide for the needs of its members, the same holds for states that entrust the public's well-being chiefly to the market. These market-facilitating states therefore implicitly make the contingent claim that the people's welfare is best served by relying chiefly on the market. This proposition assumes that the market is mere means to the general welfare as end—and that, therefore, the public's well-being is normative *for* the market, as it is for the state, and for its members in their capacity as citizens. Thus Goodin can say: "The market and the welfare state officially aim at the same end—promoting public welfare. Morally as well as economically, the fundamental justification of the market is simply

---

[11] There is no intent here to deny the usefulness of the derivative arguments. Chapter 5 of this book offers a *specific conception* of the general welfare as partly derivative of the Constitution. Such a conception will, in moral-realist fashion, be distinguished from the general concept or idea of the general welfare, or *the general welfare itself*. The latter will remain normative for the former, thus preserving what common sense affirms: the possibility of error in any concrete judgment of what actually benefits a community and its members.

that under certain, tightly specified conditions, the operations of the market will serve to maximize social welfare. That is the central tenet of modern economics, first formulated by Adam Smith."[12]

Yet viewing state and market as means to the same end is not an innocuous step; modern followers of Smith may well resist it. Norman Barry is an example. Barry is a leading student of the welfare debate and generally a critic of what he calls the modern welfare state. At one point he contrasts two "line[s] of liberal welfare thinking," one proceeding from Bentham and the other, he says contrary to Goodin, from Smith. The Benthamite tradition "depends on *knowledge*" of the sort claimed or sought by "a centralized legislator" who is prepared to "evaluate various collective 'end states'—configurations of wealth, income, well-being, and so on—in terms of their measurable welfare enhancing properties" and "to reform, intervene and correct the failings of the market" accordingly. Barry opposes such thinking. He sees "an ineradicable . . . *subjectivism* in all decisions about welfare," and he says that this subjectivism makes advance knowledge of what conduces to well-being impossible. So, for Barry, the market cannot be answerable to some conception of the general welfare, nor can some substantive theory of the general welfare justify state-initiated market reform. Barry says that despite "the use of such phrases as 'the public interest,' the rationale of the market is not that it produces any such 'knowable' outcome or final state, but that it co-ordinates human action and provides that minimal level of predictability which individuals need to secure their own well-being."[13]

The obvious response to Barry is that he assumes knowledge of the very sort he tries to deny. In effect, he conceives well-being as the individual's (sense of?) possessing the capacity and the opportunity to pursue wants that the market and market society can either supply or tolerate. And since the market is a set of socially situated practices, the wants that it either satisfies or tolerates must be perceived by anonymous others as either reasonable or harmless. I argue later that this view of well-being is inevitably a bourgeois view and thus a contentious one. Barry assumes its validity despite his vaunted moral subjectivism about the nature of well-being. Not surprisingly, therefore, he eventually puts his subjectivism aside. Later he notes with approval Hayek's conception of a welfare-enhancing policy not as one that accepts whatever the market brings but as one that increases the chances of what is silently assumed to be an objective good: higher incomes of

[12] Goodin, "Reasons for Welfare," 24.

[13] Norman Barry, *Welfare* (Minneapolis: University of Minnesota Press, 1990), 24–25, his emphasis.

persons taken at random (58–59). With this Barry concedes that "some collectivist criterion of welfare seems unavoidable even in the most individualistic of doctrines" (59). He quotes with approval Amartya Sen's view that it is hard to divorce the value of the market from the value of its results, and he asserts that compared with other systems the "liberal market economy ... has enhanced welfare" in the economic sense (ibid.). Barry thus assumes in spite of himself that some valid view of the general welfare is possible in advance of the market's results *and* that the market is answerable to that view.

I defend a strong version of this assumption in chapter 2. There I argue that the general welfare cannot be normative for any entity—market, state, or citizenry—where the general welfare is conceived solely as whatever the market's allocation turns out to be, or however some philosophic or political authority (state or citizenry) happens to define it, or as enabling whatever some political or philosophic authority conceives as effective citizenship. By some accounts citizenship may consist in no more than the bare right to vote and be counted equally with all others. Yet no one can argue that honoring this right is sufficient to transport the involuntarily homeless to a state of economic well-being. Honoring participatory rights of equal citizenship may be a step in the right direction and the only obligation of some hypothetical community. But such a community (if we could imagine it) would have little commitment to the welfare of its members. Defenders of the market state and the market society cannot help claiming, if only implicitly, that these entities constitute communities that provide for many of the important needs of their members. These claims may be held dogmatically, but they remain mere claims; people making them cannot help assuming they can prove to be false. And this assumption implies that no agent of its client's welfare can perform its duties simply by stipulating what shall count as the client's well-being. Thus the state, even a democratic state, can be wrong about what constitutes the welfare of its people.

When the implicit claim of a community to serve the well-being of its members does prove to be false, the appropriate remedy is less a matter of theory than of practical wisdom; it depends on contingencies like what parts of the claim are false, what moral or scientific facts make them false, what parts of the community care, what they are prepared to do, and what they are able to do. When markets fail, or to the extent and in the respects that market failure proves chronic, the least that can be said is that market principles cease to be normative for civic communities established to serve the needs of their members, and these communities have a reason to compensate for the market's failure. The community's refusal to vindicate its claims constitutes a rea-

son for political reform. And, in a democracy, members of the community who are materially harmed or otherwise troubled by the state's
failure can take this as a failure of the general population and therewith as reason for criticism and reform of cultural proportions. The
duties and aspirations of communities committed to the general welfare are defined neither by opinion (either authoritative or authenti-
cally popular) nor by some model of political or economic participation. They are defined by the general welfare itself or, in practice, by
what the best self-critical and reflective effort of a people continually
reveals to them about their true needs and the morally and instrumentally best ways to pursue them.

Efforts of this sort can adduce evidence that favors the market, but
because this can happen only under some conditions and in some respects, the welfare state—that is, the political community that acts on
its claim to provide for the needs of its members—is not an adjunct of
the market. It is rather the market that is an adjunct of the political
community, just as the (constitutional) state is an instrument of its
ends. These controversial propositions flow from a general conception
of the people's well-being as a fundamental end of popularly constituted government; they are elaborated and defended in this book. Before the main arguments begin, however, I'll comment on several objections to the capacious sense of welfare in Walzer's statement that
every state is in principle a welfare state.

"Welfare": How Capacious the Term?

Some readers will object to a broad sense of the term "welfare." They
will agree with Barry that a broad sense of "welfare" departs from current political usage and trivializes the welfare debate. They will point
out that the current subject of political debate is the variety and extent
of relief for the poor—"poor support" in the form of redistributive
state entitlements—not whether the political community should provide for (any of) the needs of its members.[14] My answer to this objection is simply that influential and powerful figures in the current political debate—chiefly the United States Supreme Court—in fact do deny
that the American Constitution obligates any of our governments to
serve any of the substantive needs of their people. Some conservatives
deny any and all affirmative constitutional duties precisely because, as
we shall see later in this chapter and in chapter 2, they now see that
granting the existence of even a minimal positive duty, like police pro-

---

[14] See Moon, *Responsibility, Rights, and Welfare*, 2; *cf.*, Barry, *Welfare*, 5, 33, 38.

tection against private violence, makes it harder to deny that the state is obligated to help the poor. Because these conservatives implicitly put police protection and poor support in the same boat, they implicitly sanction a capacious sense of the term "welfare."

The Supreme Court confirmed its antiwelfarist position in *DeShaney v. Winnebago County Department of Social Services* (1989).[15] In 1984 one Randy DeShaney beat his four-year-old son, Joshua, into a permanently retarded state. Because the Department of Social Services had previously been informed at least four times of DeShaney's past acts of violence against Joshua, three times by physicians attending the child in local hospitals, and because the department's caseworkers had been monitoring Joshua's case for over two years, Joshua's mother, divorced from DeShaney, brought a federal suit in Joshua's behalf against the department and some of its employees. She claimed that the department had failed to protect Joshua from what it should have known was a violent parent and that this failure denied Joshua's right to physical security under the Fourteenth Amendment. The Court dismissed the action by a vote of six to three. Chief Justice William Rehnquist wrote for the Court that since Joshua was not in the physical custody of the state at the time of his injuries, the Constitution imposed no obligation on the state to protect him from third-party violence. Citing cases denying rights to abortion funding and adequate housing, Rehnquist held that the framers "were content to leave the extent of [substantive] governmental obligation . . . to the democratic process." To this he added with approval the following statement from another case: "As a general matter, a state is under no duty to provide substantive services for those within its border."[16]

The Rehnquist Court itself has thus implicitly put governmental provision of physical security, adequate housing, and medical treatment in the same category. And by so doing it has licensed a strategy of defending poor support that begins with proving what should be an uncontroversial proposition: that the constitutional state is obligated to provide the minimal substantive benefit of the nightwatchman state,

---

[15] 489 U.S. 189 (1989).

[16] 489 U.S. 196, quoting from *Youngberg v. Romeo*, 457 U.S. 307, 317 (1982), and citing, inter alia, *Lindsey v. Normet*, 405 U.S. 56, 74 (1972) (state not constitutionally obligated to provide adequate housing) and *Harris v. McRae* 448 U.S. 297, 317–18 (1980) (Congress not constitutionally obligated to fund abortion or other medical services). Technically, *Lindsey* dealt with the due process clause of the Fourteenth Amendment and *Harris* with the due process clause of the Fifth Amendment. But these clauses served as vehicles for characterizing the Constitution as a whole, conflating it with the judicially cognizable constitution. Thus, at 489 U.S. 196, Rehnquist treated the proposition from *Youngberg* as a general principle of constitutional law.

namely, bodily security of the kind arguably denied Joshua DeShaney.
I offer proof of this obligation in chapter 2 of this book as part of a
larger contention that the American Constitution makes sense as a
charter *primarily* of benefits, and that the Constitution makes no sense
as the charter of negative liberties depicted in *DeShaney* and compan-
ion cases.

Though I regard the chief justice's argument for the Court's action
in *DeShaney* (the *argument*, not necessarily the decision, as we shall see)
a constitutional and strategic mistake, I fully accept the Court's implicitly capacious sense of governmental benefits or welfare, and I could
cite *DeShaney* as legal authority for the usage I propose. Justification
for a broad sense of "welfare" lies also in the fact that there is no clear
separation of redistributive policies from either regulatory policies or
forbearances from regulation for the sake of "negative rights." Barry
himself concedes as much, albeit with no effect on his restricted sense
of "welfare." He relates the "obvious point" that "redistribution" is involved in the state's protection for negative rights, like the "right to
life" protected by laws against murder (his example) and the institutions that enforce these laws. Enacting and enforcing these laws involves redistribution because it "involve[s] positive action by the state
in the provision of courts, police and so on." To this Barry adds a point
that Americans can well appreciate in the new age of "homeland security": that the law-and-order or nightwatchman state, "although limited, could still be very large," requiring "virtually unlimited expendi-
ture."[17] Later he says that provision for the poor can be justified as
"logically equivalent to the demand for [national] defence, law and
order and all the other familiar activities by the state," and that "to
this extent traditional [free-market] liberalism is as much a welfarist
doctrine as any other political ideology" (119).

Barry thus suggests that all acts of government are either immediately redistributive or protective of prior redistributive acts. An extensive case for this proposition is set forth by Stephen Holmes and Cass
Sunstein in a recent book that draws out implications of the fact that
the protection of so-called negative rights depends on governments
that are "to extract and reallocate" money and other resources from
those who have to those who have not.[18] Holmes and Sunstein invite

---

[17] Barry, *Welfare*, 79.

[18] Holmes and Sunstein, *The Cost of Rights*, 29–39; see also 62–64, 114–17, 129, 131, 165,
184–88, 216, 230. For some of the earlier versions of this point, see Graber, "Clintonification
of American Law," 760–62. See also Bandes, "The Negative Constitution," 2282–85, 2323–
25. At one point Barry classifies welfare policies as either redistributive or actuarial (forms
of social insurance). Though he wants to claim that the latter is largely consistent with free-
market ideology (see 92, 101, 104–5), he eventually observes that "in almost all cases the

persons who think they oppose poor support as a matter of principle to "contemplate the obvious": that the definition and protection of property is a "government service" to the propertied funded from "general revenues extracted from the public at large" (29). They add that like all government services, this one is justified only to the extent that it contributes to "collective purposes," in this case the "nation's real estate and capital stock" (116–17).

To critics who might contend that unlike the poor, the propertied create the wealth that funds their own support, Holmes and Sunstein point to the dependence of property and the market on such state functions as national defense and on the contributions of "low-income youth" whom the state conscripts in times of war (62–63). Critics of Holmes and Sunstein may respond that conscription should not count as redistribution because victory in war is a public good from which all Americans benefit equally, even though some Americans might regard some wars as immoral and even illegal. But a similar argument can justify state provision for the poor. If all Americans arguably could have benefited from an American military victory, say, in Vietnam, notwithstanding the many Americans who opposed that war and the number who even urged and ultimately applauded victory by the other side, why could not all Americans have benefited from the successes of tax-supported campaigns against poverty? If conscription for foreign wars does not count as some pejorative form of redistribution, why view taxation for the War on Poverty as a pejorative form of redistribution? And if both forms of war are redistributive and wrong solely because redistributive, we have graduated to a general moral philosophy that condemns all coercive government, including democratic governments that redistribute resources to protect so-called negative liberties. I need not ask how one could justify such a theory. (Or how one could even state such a theory: Can property be so individualized and the right thereto so strong as to condemn the redistribution needed to define and enforce laws against theft—i.e., theft of property?) It is enough for me to note that exercises in normative constitutional theory must assume the possible legitimacy of constitutional government and therewith—since constitutional government, is still *government*, and since government is necessarily redistributive—the difficulty of condemning redistribution per se.

As a term of everyday political discourse, "welfare" does refer to state provision for the poor, the elderly, and the disabled. But "welfare" is hardly limited to such references even in ordinary political dis-

---

insurance element quickly becomes a fiction and the services become, to all intents and purposes, tax financed," the benefits "of *redistributive* taxation" (115, his emphasis).

course. A broader use is evident in such familiar expressions as "corporate welfare," "middle-class entitlements," and, more interestingly, "the general welfare."[19] Barry himself cites social-scientific findings and a "'theorem' of political economy known as 'Director's Law'" in observing the tendency of all Western democracies to redistribute toward middle-income groups more than to the poor, a pattern reversible, he says, only by a "most unlikely alliance between rich and poor."[20] Regarding "the general welfare," general readers are likely to find no profound substantive conflict among Madison's statements that "Justice is the end of government" (51:352) and that "the public good, the real welfare of the great body of the people is the supreme object to be pursued; and that no form of government whatever, has any other value, than as it may be fitted for the attainment of this object" (45:309). There is no evidence that this juxtaposition of statements would have been unintelligible to Madison or to his audience, and it may owe its intelligibility to us by virtue of what Barry calls the "promiscuity of welfare" as "a concept which attaches itself indiscriminately to other moral and political ideas," especially justice.[21]

Barry treats the "promiscuity of welfare" as a cause of error and "confusion in political argument," chiefly with regard to the rank ordering of political ends. Attaching welfare to justice and other ends evidently gives welfare a preeminence that Barry wants to deny. He would "disentangle" welfare from justice, rights, and social order, first

---

[19] Listing such benefits risks being construed as a concession to the false distinction between redistributive and nonredistributive policies. Nevertheless, I refer the reader to a biting exposé of what the authors call government "wealthfare," or "the money we hand out to corporations and wealthy individuals," some $488 billion a year as of 1996; see Mark Zepezaur and Arthur Naiman, *Take the Rich Off Welfare* (Tucson, Ariz.: Odonian Press, 1996).

[20] Barry, *Welfare*, 106–7.

[21] Ibid., 6. In three contiguous sentences of *Federalist* No. 45 (309), Publius conflates "the public good," "the real welfare of the great body of the people," and "the public happiness." At the risk of illustrating Barry's point about the "promiscuity of welfare," I follow Publius's lead in this book. Though I appreciate ways in which people can be well-off without being happy, lack of analytic refinement in this particular is of no consequence in the present debate. In chapter 2 I show that the Constitution is a scheme for reconciling public opinion to the public's true well-being. Constitutional government at its ideal best must therefore bring public opinion as far as it can be brought toward the public's true well-being. Or, in the alternative, constitutional government should pursue the closest approximation of the general welfare that the public can approve. In either case constitutional government will strive for an overlap between some approximation of the general welfare as an objective good and the public's subjective well-being. And there is a sense of happiness (a sober, reflective happiness) that makes happiness and subjective well-being working surrogates of each other. This excuses Publius's conflation of the public happiness and the public welfare.

asserting that welfare "intuitively has no greater claim to priority" and eventually suggesting it be ranked lower than the rest. He complains that a conception of welfare broad enough to link welfare with justice effectively undermines the distinction between (welfare as) *redistributive entitlements* and (justice as) *the negative virtue of not hurting others in possessions they have lawfully acquired.* And, he adds, where welfare and rights are connected, (rights as) "claims to forbearance from invasive actions by others" excuse (welfare as) "entitlements to well-being from the state" (5–6).

I have supplied parentheticals in the last two sentences to show that Barry's complaint about a broad sense of "welfare" is little more than a complaint; as an argument it is a poor one because it begs the question. Even if valid in the welfare context (we have seen otherwise), a distinction between helping people through redistributive entitlements and trying to prevent people from hurting each other, cannot by itself argue for limiting either "welfare" to "redistributive entitlements" or "justice" to "not hurting others." The same holds for Barry's distinction between claims to "forbearance" from invasive harms and claims to "entitlements." That distinction, by itself, falls short of justifying any given use of the term "rights." If confusion of distinct things is all we would avoid, why not reserve "rights" for "redistributive entitlements"? And if the answer is that people generally attach value to "rights" that we do not want attached to "entitlements, " it can only be because there is something wrong with entitlements, which has to be shown. Whether "welfare" should be conceived exclusively as redistributive entitlements; whether justice can be conceived solely as a negative virtue; whether the state does much of anything, if anything at all, that does not require redistribution of resources; whether rights can be conceived (much less honored in practice) apart from redistributive practices—all these positions must be argued for.

Barry offers what he thinks are reasons for disconnecting welfare from justice and rights. He proposes two such reasons: first, that "disentangling . . . welfare from other values" serves to clarify political language "so that value disagreements can be more easily identified," and second—explicitly his main concern—that "the assimilation of other values to the welfare ideal imposes upon a society an agreement about values, an hierarchy of ends and purposes, which is unlikely to exist." Barry bases this second claim partly on the controversies regarding the meaning of "'well-being' . . . and other familiar expressions of welfare philosophy." He is confident that these "intractable disputes" will lead to "little or no convergence" of opinion, even among those who agree that "welfare should be the goal of public policy" (6–7).

The first of these reasons (clarity of language) makes for effective
argument only where inquiry seeks to disassociate kinds of things
whose association is admitted by all sides to be a mistake. Where there
is no such admission, the argument assumes what has to be shown.
Chapter 2 of this book contends that the state's provision of resources
for ends like justice and order is itself a contribution to the general
welfare that the state is constitutionally obligated to make. The chapter
contends further that the duty to provide for justice, order, and the
security of persons and property through police protection, courts of
civil and criminal justice, and other means argues for duties to combat
or relieve poverty and disability. This book thus argues for the broad,
connected view of welfare and welfare provision that Barry opposes.
What he and others might count as a purification of political discourse
I would therefore count as a distortion of political reality, and I shall
try to defend my account.

As for Barry's principal suggestion regarding usage, it is not evident
why a broad, connected view of welfare and welfare provision should
either impose values on society or encourage the imposition of values
on society. It is hard to see what is especially impositional about usage
that recognizes the redistributive nature of, say, the civil enforcement
of contracts. Who is imposed upon by references to "corporate welfare," a term whose use acknowledges the fact of direct and indirect
corporate subsidies? I presume here that Barry would probably agree
that values can fairly be said to be imposed on society only when stable
majorities of citizens have no realistic hope of lawfully changing particular governmental policies and procedures. The question would
then be why Barry assumes that a broad, connected view of welfare
should invite undemocratic imposition more so than a restricted view
of welfare, which, under some circumstances, a stable majority might
also oppose to no avail because of the strategic advantages of a well-
situated minority. The current lack of a prescription drug benefit under
Medicare can thus be seen as an imposition on the majority of the population whose taxes help pay for the legal, physical, and social preconditions of the pharmaceutical industry that, so far, has successfully opposed the proposed entitlement. Even if corporate welfare and poor
relief combined were somehow more impositional than corporate welfare without poor relief (the latter affecting a minority that is poor, the
former a majority composed of the poor and the stockholding middle
and upper classes), where is the imposition in merely labeling corporate subsidies and poor relief what they seem to be: varieties of state
provision or "welfare"?

Though Barry omits explanation, part of the answer to this last question may lie, ironically, in the most likely justification *for* a broad view

of welfare. Chapter 2 of this book borrows from writers like Holmes and Sunstein to argue that the provision of, say, police and courts should count as provisions for the general welfare and that granting that government has these obligations leaves no principled way to deny at least some governmental help for the poor.[22] If this argument proves to be sound, some help for the poor is morally and constitutionally imperative for all who agree that the state is constitutionally obligated to provide for police and courts. Implicit agreement with this proposition is one way to explain Rehnquist's denial of Wisconsin's obligation to protect Joshua DeShaney from predictable violence. For those who cannot deny this obligation—an undeniable obligation, argues chapter 2—our hypothesis puts the force of constitutional principle behind state provision for the poor; it removes active concern for the poor from the sphere of discretionary political choice. Chief Justice Charles Evans Hughes affirmed this imperative of a decent society in his celebrated approval of a Depression era minimum-wage law: "What ... workers lose in wages" from "unconscionable employers," said Hughes, "the taxpayers are called upon to pay. The bare cost of living must be met."[23]

If imposition lurks in such an argument, it lies in the imperatives of moral and, I shall argue, constitutional principle. As construed here and in recent works by most constitutional theorists presently defending a constitutional duty of welfare provision, this duty authorizes no unconditional *judicial* impositions on unwilling politicians and taxpayers.[24] (Hughes and the Court upheld a minimum wage enacted by a state legislature; they did not impose the minimum wage by judicial decree.) Even if judicially unenforceable, the duty in question would justify exhortation and criticism of the electorate and its representatives in the Constitution's name, exhortation and criticism perhaps by judges (depending on a relaxation of the judge-made rule against "advisory opinions") and certainly by others. The others include constitutional theorists; they would be concerned with constitutional ends as they now are with institutions and negative liberties.

Our question thus becomes whether an imperative of constitutional principle counts as an (illegitimate) imposition on democracy. Another

---

[22] See Holmes, *Passions and Constraint*, 245–46.

[23] *West Coast Hotel Co. v. Parrish*, 300 U.S. 379, 399 (1937).

[24] See Sager, "Justice in Plain Clothes," 420–25; Sunstein, *Partial Constitution*, 139, 145–49; Michelman, "Welfare Rights in a Constitutional Democracy," 684–85. For an exception, see Graber, "Clintonification of American Law," 753–62. See also Bandes, "The Negative Constitution," 2327–30. I qualify my reservations about judicial power in the concluding section of chapter 6, which discusses the special problem of constitutional failure.

way to put this question is whether democracy can be reconciled to constitutionalism or whether democracy can take constitutional form. I assume here that democracy can take constitutional form partly because I have defended the proposition elsewhere, partly because I think relatively few readers of this book expect the question reopened here, and partly because the argument here is offered as an exercise in the normative theory of constitutional democracy, an exercise that must assume the legitimacy and possibility of constitutional democracy. For these reasons an appeal to democracy *against* constitutionalism belongs to a different debate.[25] Barry's second argument is out of place in the present discussion. Barry's argument from the impositional character of welfare broadly conceived could be relevant here only if the imperatives of moral and constitutional principle constitute illegitimate impositions on popular majorities, for the imperative of moral-constitutional principle is the only imperative in the connected view of "welfare" that Barry opposes.

An exercise in first-order constitutional theory, this book is an inquiry whose findings are submitted to a more-or-less democratic readership that attaches normative weight to constitutional principles. Exercises of this sort must assume that constitutional imperatives are not illegitimately impositional. If a capacious view of "welfare" is wrong in the present context, the reason must be not that it imposes anything on anyone but that it does so illegitimately—that is, that it defeats some constitutional purpose or offends some constitutional principle. It could be, for example, that usage which lumps poor support with police protection undermines the general welfare by trying to put a form of unproductive state provision in legitimate company. Such an argument would turn on the proposition that redistributive state provision for the poor (or whomever) actually harms everyone, including its recipients. This is a familiar contention against poor support, and I can safely assume here that it is at least partly or even largely correct. My present concern is not the soundness of this particular case against poor support but its general argumentative character. The proposition that poor support actually hurts the poor hardly implies that government has no obligation to facilitate their welfare; it may in fact function as the premise of what is formally a welfarist argument.

Charles Murray makes such a welfarist argument. He says the nation should abandon "the state social insurance and welfare apparatus" of the modern state, including "every middle-class entitlement,

---

[25] For my contribution to this debate, see Sotirios A. Barber, *The Constitution of Judicial Power* (Baltimore: Johns Hopkins University Press, 1993), esp. chaps. 2, 7.

agricultural subsidy, and corporate subsidy along with programs for the poor."[26] These schemes, he says, foster irresponsibility among their supposed beneficiaries by trying to insulate them from the painful consequences that naturally follow upon their conduct. The result? "The babies of the poor languish. Poor people . . . huddle in cardboard boxes beneath overpasses. The rich install ever more sophisticated security systems around their estates" (130–34). Murray's cure? Abolish most transfer programs and limit the state largely to preventing private violence, providing for the limited number of public purposes that include national defense and an educated population (private education funded through state vouchers), *and* "enabling people to enter into enforceable voluntary agreements" (7–10, 12, 95–97). This last function of course secures "the right of contract and the edifice of law" that constitute the modern market, and it is freedom to function responsibly in this market that will eventually secure "the happiness of all the people" (9, 130). This argument is a welfarist argument. It assumes that the constitutional state is obligated to do what it reasonably can to facilitate the people's well-being.

Yet one final argument can be made for Barry's view that imposition lurks in welfare broadly conceived: For those who hold that the Constitution demands some state provision for the poor, it becomes all but impossible to avoid at least *some* judicial impositions, or the appearance thereof, on popular majorities who might disagree with judicial readings of the Constitution. Even if it is left to popular legislatures to decide initially what benefits go immediately to whom and at whose immediate expense, affirmative legislative decisions could create openings for judicial action under the judicially enforceable principle that the state should provide equal protection of the laws. Thus, everyone understands that courts could act against a state's policy of extending police protection only to white Protestant heterosexuals, for the defect of such a policy would be its discriminatory character, not its failure to provide a benefit. Conceive police protection as just another form of redistributive welfare and it is not inconceivable that some judges might reason from police protection to "welfare rights." The argument would be that having initially decided to take liberty and other resources from some persons (the strong and bold) to benefit others (the weak and timid) who disproportionately need police protection, the principle of equal protection requires that the legislature take from

[26] Charles Murray, *What It Means to Be a Libertarian* (New York: Broadway Books, 1997), 130.

some (the rich) to meet the disproportionate need of others (the poor) for education, housing, and medical care.[27]

Though this last argument would be a startling departure from current judicial doctrine, it could conceivably take hold at some future point. Add further premises to this prospect, and you could challenge my claims that constitutional democrats as such cannot view constitutional principles as illegitimately impositional and that constitutionalizing welfare need not mean more power for unelected judges. If constitutional meaning were in the eye of the beholder (something I have denied elsewhere)[28], if judicial findings of "welfare rights" went against popular conceptions of constitutional meaning, and if elected institutions were staffed and organized as fairly to represent the public's preferences better than the courts, then Barry might be right: relatively undemocratic imposition might lurk in a broad sense of the term "welfare." But a crucial element of this challenge is the premise that constitutional meaning is in the eye of the beholder; this premise expresses a moral metaphysics that finds the meaning of normative terms like "the general welfare" and "equal protection" in some subjective source. Barry is quite open about his moral subjectivism, as we have seen. The principal weakness of this stance is that it can say nothing about the philosophic status of "welfare" and "equal protection" that would not apply also to ideas like "liberty" and "democracy," and yet it assumes both the real existence and the approximate knowability of liberty and democracy while denying the same of welfare and equal protection. When Barry says the meaning of welfare is subjective and that a broad sense of "welfare" invites imposition, he assumes there is something objectively wrong with imposition, which in turn assumes the possibility of objective truth about the moral status and meaning of liberty and democracy. He apparently does not believe, therefore, that the status and meaning of *all* moral ideas are incorrigibly subjective. And the question is, what is so specially defective about either "welfare" or "equal protection," the likely vehicle for welfare's judicial imposition? I say more about issues of this sort in chapter 4.

[27] For a partial survey of writers who adopt strategies of this kind, see Graber, "Clintonification of American Law," 753–56.

[28] Barber, *Constitution of Judicial Power*, 45–48, 203–8.

CHARTER OF NEGATIVE LIBERTIES: ARGUMENTS FROM TEXT AND HISTORY

MOST constitutional scholars conceive the American Constitution as guaranteeing only two kinds of rights: rights as exemptions from state power and rights to have one's preferences represented in the state's processes of decision, primarily the legislative process. This is the negative-liberties model of the Constitution. The model allows for state-provided substantive benefits, but only as matters of legislative or popular choice, not as matters of constitutional right (judicially enforceable or not) that government has a duty to provide or facilitate. By contrast, a benefits model of the Constitution does number substantive benefits among government's constitutional obligations. By a benefits model, Wisconsin had a *constitutional duty* to make every reasonable effort to protect Joshua DeShaney from physical violence.

Several kinds of argument support the negative-liberties model: arguments from the constitutional text and historical intent, moral arguments, metaethical arguments, and arguments from unwanted consequences. Individually and in combination, these are bad arguments. Their failings include incoherence, offense to the presuppositions of ordinary moral and political life, and failure to account for undeniable aspects of the constitutional document and the nation's constitutional experience. Though these arguments presuppose each other in part and overlap at several points, I analyze them separately here to the extent that I can. This chapter takes up the arguments from constitutional text and historical intent. Chapter 3 examines arguments from unwanted consequences, and chapter 4 discusses the moral and metaethical arguments.

IS POSITIVE CONSTITUTIONALISM AHISTORICAL?

In a widely cited defense of the negative-liberties view of the Constitution, David Currie, the renowned constitutional historian, concedes that the United States Supreme Court can find affirmative governmental duties implicit in some constitutional guarantees, as did the German Constitutional Court in a 1975 antiabortion decision and at least two other cases. Although Germany's Basic Law protects a "right to life" expressly against government only, the Constitutional Court found the fetus a person and declared it protected by a duty to criminalize abortion.[1] It thus found a guarantee against state action to imply the state's duty to restrain a species of private conduct. In another case the Constitutional Court moved beyond state prohibition of harm by third parties to read negatively phrased guarantees against government to mandate a state-provided education for all Germans. Currie conceives this benefit as protection against certain "adverse physical or economic conditions" (871–72).

By contrast, the United States Supreme Court has refused to affirm not only a Federal constitutional duty to offer children an education but even, as we saw in *DeShaney*, a Federal constitutional duty to protect children from predictable physical harm by parents whom the state knows to be abusive.[2] Lower federal courts have also declared no constitutional right to police and fire protection—no right, in effect, to the minimal guarantees of the nightwatchman state.[3] Currie approves all such results as a matter of constitutional law on textual and historical grounds. Madison and the other framers, says Currie, were not modern social democrats, and the Bill of Rights and the Fourteenth Amendment expressly proscribe governmental action only, not private action or harms caused by impersonal natural or economic forces (865–66, 877–78, 880–86).

Though Currie cites the text of the Fourteenth Amendment, which has been read by the Court to proscribe forms of state action only, not purely private conduct, his is essentially a historical, not a textual, argument. Currie acknowledges that, as in the cited German cases, a negatively phrased text can be read to guarantee positive benefits. He knows that the Fourteenth Amendment does not have to be read to proscribe governmental action only. And he knows that reading the amendment implicitly to proscribe private conduct is reading it to empower government to prevent or punish the private conduct proscribed. "Although none of the prohibitory clauses of the amendment speaks directly to private action," says Currie in another work, "[a] strong argument can be made, on the basis of the origins of the equal protection clause" (i.e., Congress's concern with unaddressed private

---

[1] Currie, "Positive and Negative Constitutional Rights," 867–72.

[2] *San Antonio v. Rodriguez*, 411 U.S. 1, 33–35 (1973); *DeShaney v. Winnebago*, 489 U.S. 189 (1989).

[3] *Jackson v. Joliet*, 715 F.2d 1200, 1204 (7th Cir. 1983); *Jackson v. Byrne*, 738 F.2d 1443, 1446 (7th Cir. 1984).

violence against blacks in the Reconstruction South) that the clause "seems to impose upon the states a unique duty to take affirmative action to protect black persons from private attack."[4] Thus, the text of the equal protection clause has been read as a federal guarantee, first, that the states *will* protect persons from unspecified forms of harm, and, second, that the states will protect persons equally.[5]

Currie sees an argument for affirmative guarantees also in the Fourteenth Amendment's promise of due process of law. He acknowledges strong historical and philosophic authority for reading the Constitution to include affirmative rights, namely, the political philosophy of John Locke, which, says Currie, "pervaded early American political thought."[6] Locke's theory "entails a surrender of the right of self-help in exchange [for] governmental protection not only of property but [also] of life and liberty," says Currie, and if the due process clauses "embody this vision, it may not be amiss to conclude . . . that they require affirmative governmental protection of life and liberty." A court, says Currie, might therefore "be tempted to conclude that a government that deprives people of life by not punishing murder also does so by declining to feed the hungry, and [with this conclusion] we would have discovered a constitutional right to basic welfare services" (877–78).

Though Currie readily agrees that inferring positive rights from Lockean principles is both a "logical step" and an interpretive possibility, he rejects the move nonetheless as a "profoundly ahistorical" departure from the nightwatchman theory of government that, he says, prevailed at both the founding and Reconstruction periods. (878) Currie thus assumes a general rule of constitutional interpretation to the effect that the framers' putative expectations should defeat admittedly logical and even commonsensical extensions of their principles. This would be a rule of interpretation that almost no contemporary originalist would avow.[7] It is hard to maintain an interpretive stance that, taken seriously, would force the national government to seek constitutional amendments before regulating interstate movements of trucks, planes, and trains as vehicles the framers did not have concretely in mind when approving governmental powers over commerce. And a sense of this difficulty could be a factor in Currie's eventual proposal

[4] David P. Currie, *The Constitution in the Supreme Court: The First Hundred Years, 1789–1888* (Chicago: University of Chicago Press, 1985), 397.

[5] See, e.g., West, "Rights, Capabilities and the Good Society," 1911–12.

[6] Currie, "Positive and Negative Constitutional Rights," 877. This part of Currie's article resonates with Justice Brennan's dissent in *DeShaney* at 489 U.S. 208–10, 212.

[7] See Barber, *Constitution of Judicial Power*, chap. 4.

that, as a theoretical matter, the Constitution excludes even the states' obligation to punish murder.[8]

This proposal—no constitutional duty to punish murder—is a very costly one for Currie, for aside from its troubling moral and political character, it contradicts Currie's views regarding Locke's influence in America (and Locke's reasons for surrendering to the state the executive power of the state of nature) and the concrete historical intentions behind the Fourteenth Amendment (regarding unaddressed private violence against blacks). It also contradicts his view of the nightwatchman theory of the founding and Reconstruction, a duty to punish murder being perhaps the first duty of the nightwatchman state.[9] Currie initially seems willing to suffer these costs for the sake of the one thing that his proposal gains for him: removing an argument for "welfare rights." But Currie quickly backs away from this radical position. Living without a nightwatchman is apparently as difficult as living with an extreme originalism, and Currie blinks when he says the state's "refusing altogether to forbid murder or theft . . . is hardly a realistic possibility" and that "in the modern world it is almost as unthinkable for a state to abandon welfare payments as to stop punishing crime" (881, 882). This concession may rescue Currie from the practical consequences of a theoretical extreme, but it wrecks his position on positive rights. If leaving crime unpunished is indeed unthinkable, Currie has no principled way to foreclose what he calls the "logical step" from the most basic forms of police protection to at least some forms of state provision for the poor.

Currie is obviously right to pull back from a pure negative-liberties model. The model may not be literally "unthinkable." A follower of Thomas Hobbes might allow that rational actors can obey a government on the strength of benefits it is expected, though not obligated, to produce.[10] But a Hobbesian view of government's obligations seems unavailable to negative libertarians who seek arguments consistent with constitutionalist assumptions. Hobbes is no constitutionalist; he disallows the defining feature of the negative-liberties constitution: ex-

[8] Currie, "Positive and Negative Constitutional Rights," 869, 881.

[9] See Murray, *What It Means to Be a Libertarian*, 7–8, 41. See also West, "Rights, Capabilities and the Good Society," 1901. West surveys liberal thinkers from Locke to Rawls and Nozick and concludes that "there may be *no* important classical liberal theorist . . . prior to . . . Robert Nozick . . . that insists on the tie between rights and negativity that has become such an entrenched part of the contemporary American constitutional mindset." This includes Isaiah Berlin, who saw the state obligated to "ensure . . . a threshold level of minimal well-being" (1910–11, citing Isaiah Berlin, *Four Essays on Liberty* [London: Oxford University Press, 1969], 123–24, 164–65, 169).

[10] See *Leviathan*, II, xviii.

emptions from power in the form of constitutional rights against the state. And the negative libertarian who would assume a Hobbesian stance against affirmative constitutional duties would have to explain how rational constitution makers could (1) establish a government (in Hobbesian fashion) for the sake of security from private violence; (2) try (in libertarian fashion) to impose restraints on that government in behalf of rights; yet (3) not try to impose an affirmative duty to secure the benefit for which the government is established.

One can argue that as *The Federalist* opposes a constitutional list of exemptions from power (84:575–81), a rational constitution maker can oppose *specifying* or *enumerating* positive constitutional rights. I show in chapter 5 that specifying positive benefits under the Fourteenth Amendment is largely unnecessary and to some extent even inconsistent with the Constitution's positive nature. My point for now, however, is that a faithful Hobbesian will not argue for what negative libertarians argue for. She cannot approve negative constitutional liberties while rejecting a right to protection against physical violence; she cannot accept the Court's opinion in *DeShaney.* Barry might disagree. He says Hobbes's "major concerns were political obligation and the theories of law and sovereignty," not "the maximization of welfare."[11] Barry could go on to argue, in the manner, say, of Lon Fuller or John Hart Ely, for a list of negative liberties conceptually connected to the idea of law and to the American idea of (*popular*) sovereignty.[12] This list could easily include rights to procedural due process, equal protection for some historically "insular minorities," the rights to vote and be counted, and therewith freedoms of speech and conscience. (Barry might or might not extend this line of thought to "penumbral" rights of privacy, though of course he would not run it to the *substantive* prerequisites of meaningful and equal citizenship.) So our neo-Hobbesian, reasoning from Barry's account of Hobbes's major concerns, might end up with the *DeShaney* majority after all.

But Hobbes does not separate his putative concerns (sovereignty, political obligation) from substantive goods the way Barry does. Many writers, from Aristotle and Marx to modern social scientists like Pivin and Cloward, have commented on the connection between helping the poor and keeping the lid on domestic disorder; Barry notes this connection at one point.[13] This connection is merely contingent, however,

---

[11] Barry, *Welfare*, 7.

[12] See John Hart Ely, *Democracy and Distrust: A Theory of Judicial Review* (Cambridge: Harvard University Press, 1980), chap. 4; Lon L. Fuller, *The Morality of Law* (New Haven, Conn.: Yale University Press, 1964), 102–6.

[13] See Francis Fox Pivin and Richard A. Cloward, *Regulating the Poor: The Functions of Public Welfare* (New York: Vintage Books, 1993), chap. 1; Barry, *Welfare*, 41.

and Hobbes suggests a much stronger link between at least one substantive good and his concerns with law and sovereignty. Like Joshua DeShaney's mother, Hobbes's contracting subject looks to the sovereign to protect her and her child from violence at the hands of third parties. And where the sovereign itself withholds that protection or threatens her life, Hobbes excuses her from further obligation to the sovereign.[14] For the Hobbesian subject, therefore, obligation to the sovereign ceases when the sovereign disconnects itself from physical security, the end for which the subject originally sought and agreed to leave the war of all against all in the state of nature. Hobbes's theory of political obligation and the origin (or end) of government enables a positive constitutionalist like Stephen Holmes to cite him in a brief for the welfare state. Holmes describes the liberal tradition that stretches from Hobbes to the New Deal as concerned chiefly with combating "sources of insecurity." Security, he says, justified absolute sovereignty (for Hobbes) under conditions of civil war and anarchy, and security justified welfare liberalism (for Roosevelt) when the market itself became a source of insecurity.[15]

Hobbesian possibilities aside pending their further elaboration, the negative model may also describe constitutions that take the form of written restrictions on preexisting governments, as did Magna Charta. Hamilton suggests this in *Federalist* No. 84 when he argues that a bill of rights is more appropriately a restraint on monarchy than on popularly established governments (578). But the negative model cannot account for all that American-style constitutions do. American constitutions specify, arrange, and provide for the staffing of offices and institutions. They also authorize types of institutional acts in functional terms like "executive" and "judicial." In addition, they authorize kinds of legislation often in specific substantive terms, as in the powers to "regulate commerce," "coin money and regulate the value thereof," and prohibit "involuntary servitude, except as a punishment for crime."

Authorizations like these are most plausibly understood as they have always been understood: as envisioning such goods as a free labor force, a national market, a stable currency—and therewith, plausibly, a national prosperity in which all responsible persons can share.[16] Hamilton contended in *Federalist* No. 84 (578–79) that these institutions and enabling grants of power were the essentials of the American Constitution and that exemptions from power in the form of specified

[14] See *Leviathan*, II, xxi.

[15] Holmes, *Passions and Constraint*, 257–58.

[16] Sotirios A. Barber, *On What the Constitution Means* (Baltimore: Johns Hopkins University Press, 1984), 71–77.

rights were unnecessary and perhaps even dangerous. The least to be said here is that exemptions from power presuppose power, and power publicly proposed and defended, and popularly established and "ordained," implicitly promises benefits. The political campaign for ratification made the promise of benefits explicit for the founding generation. The Constitution's Preamble makes this promise explicit for subsequent generations. And though preambles may not be sources of law for courts to apply, no one will deny that they can establish the basic normative properties of the enactments they introduce. Hamilton assumed as much when he cited the positive language of the Preamble as "a better recognition of popular rights than volumes of those aphorisms which make the principal figure in several of our state bills of rights" (84:578–79).

For the negative-liberties model to describe a government established through public deliberation, some justification must be found for a government whose sole duties would be disconnected from its purposes. Its *duties* (marked by negative liberties) would be forms of not acting, like not acting in ways that abridge speech. Its *purposes* would be ends like national security and prosperity. We could not understand its duties (forms of not acting) as its sole purposes, however, for the same reason that we could not understand a machine invented for the sole purpose of not doing something. Such an (act of) establishment would indeed be unthinkable.[17]

We should not be surprised, therefore, to find much historical evidence against Currie's account of welfare and the founding. This evidence includes a general view of government that admits redistributive provision for the poor. Arguments for such provision are found in classical liberal writers from Montesquieu, Hume, and Locke to Smith and Madison.[18] Walter Trattner describes redistributive efforts for relieving forms of poverty that began in England at least as far back as the Poor Law of 1601, which prefigured similar enactments in Plymouth Colony in 1642, Virginia in 1646, Connecticut in 1673, and Massachusetts in 1692.[19] Though Trattner (19–24) regards aspects of these local laws (corporal punishment of able-bodied vagabonds, apprenticeship of children, brutal exclusion of nonresidents) as paternalistic

---

[17] For how this point figured in the debate between Federalists and Anti-Federalists over a bill of rights, see Herbert J. Storing, *What the Anti-Federalists Were For* (Chicago: University of Chicago Press, 1981), 67–69. For acknowledgment of this point by an influential theorist of the American Right, see Richard A. Epstein, *Takings: Private Property and the Power of Eminent Domain* (Cambridge: Harvard University Press, 1985), 107–8.

[18] Sunstein, *Partial Constitution*, 137–41; Holmes, *Passions and Constraint*, 243–63.

[19] Walter L. Trattner, *From Poor Law to Welfare State: A History of Social Welfare in America* (New York: Free Press, 1974), 10–11, 17–18.

and inhumane by present standards, he also says they provided adequate levels of food, lodging, clothing, and medical care for less fortunate but "worthy" neighbors.[20] Reinforced by private philanthropy, these programs were motivated partly by a religious duty to help the destitute and partly by the Enlightenment's emphasis on human equality and reasonableness and a capacity for social planning and reform.[21]

Trattner reports that by the mid–eighteenth century municipalities throughout the colonies were spending from 10 to 35 percent of their revenues on welfare relief—their "single largest annual outlay" (30). He goes on to describe how this "age of humanitarianism" in America was reinforced by the Revolution, which

> intensified the sense of humanitarianism and reform that had already gripped many Americans. The Declaration of Independence, with its emphasis on reason and equality, naturally tended to call attention to the need to improve the common man's lot. Moreover, independence in the New World, where resources were abundant, offered Americans the opportunity, if not obligation, to root out old errors and vices and erect a society which would be a beacon to the world. At the very least, if the independent republic and democratic rule were to endure, American citizens had to be exempt from such impediments as illiteracy, poverty, and distress so that they could cast their ballots freely and rationally. (37)

The story is complicated in the Revolution's aftermath by the increasing separation of church and state, social dislocations that called for statewide attacks on what had previously been treated as a local problem, the economic opportunities presented by a wider frontier, a resulting emphasis on individual self-sufficiency, and an emphasis on states' rights and a limited federal role in domestic affairs (37–42).

These later developments preclude a smooth and unqualified connection between the American founding and the Great Society of the 1960s. But the proposition that government has a duty to relieve the suffering of the poor is an old one that survived even the heyday of market ideology at the end of the nineteenth century. Michael Katz reports that the spread of industrial capitalism in the North and capitalist agriculture in the postwar South exacerbated the effects of the business cycle and increasingly divided the nation along class lines. As fear of black assertiveness grew in the white South, business leaders prepared to confront city dwellers seeking relief. Not only were the latter in-

---

[20] For an even more favorable view of these early forms of poor relief and the philosophy behind them, see Marvin Olasky, *The Tragedy of American Compassion* (Wheaton, Ill.: Crossway Books, 1992), chaps. 1, 13.

[21] Trattner, *From Poor Law to Welfare State*, 34–37.

creasing at "an alarming rate," says Katz, "many of them had learned to regard relief as a right, not as an act of charity." Business and its allies in government and elsewhere met these threats with measures that ranged from military force against striking workers to a propaganda campaign against the claims of the poor.[22]

Katz says that one element of this campaign was the "theory of scientific charity." The chief targets of this theory were the systems of outdoor relief that had been established in a number of American cities, "indiscriminate" forms of public and private charity (i.e., relief that did not seek the economic and moral rehabilitation of the able-bodied poor), and the claim that relief was a right or entitlement (69). Katz credits the principal American statement of scientific charity to Josephine Shaw Lowell, a New England socialite.[23]

Lowell began her argument, in *Public Relief and Private Charity* (1884), with a strong statement against the case for poor support at public expense. She wrote that because "[t]he public funds are always somebody's money," and more often not of the few but of "the many, who are struggling to keep or to obtain their own homes, and to whom a slight increase or decrease [in taxes] is a great matter," it is wrong "to take money by law from one man and give it to another, unless for the benefit of both." From this Lowell reasoned that "the policy of public poor relief . . . can be justified" only if "it is better both for those who are so fed and maintained, and for those who supply the food and maintenance."[24] She expressed equal sympathy for the view that public relief was compulsory on taxpayers and that compulsory relief "in all its forms" undermined the common good by removing incentives to "prudence and industry" and by "diminishing the rewards of industry and forethought." But despite her appreciation of the case against state provision for the poor, Lowell seemed more impressed with the contrary view. Though arguments against compulsory relief "are undoubtedly right in the abstract," she said, they ignore additional points, including "the benefit to the whole people" when public relief prevents violence that results from "the absolute pressure of want." They also disregard the "imperative" nature of "human pity" that "would open every hand" to those asking for "food and money . . . on the ground that they were starving" (2–3).

---

[22] Michael B. Katz, *In the Shadow of the Poorhouse: A Social History of Welfare in America* (New York: Basic Books, 1996), 69.

[23] Ibid., 72. For a similar assessment of Lowell's influence, see Olasky, *Tragedy of American Compassion*, 77.

[24] Josephine Shaw Lowell, *Public Relief and Private Charity* (New York: Arno Press and The New York Times, 1971), 1–2.

Lowell built on this last observation to assert as a "postulate" (67–68) that "will scarcely be denied by anyone" (3) that, "if possible, all members of any civilized community must live" and thus "must be maintained by the produce of those who work" (67–68). This statement expressed the same thought that was to appear in Chief Justice Hughes's statement in *Parrish* some fifty years later: "The bare cost of living must be met." And this imperative of both morality and prudence left Lowell asking not whether to redistribute wealth to help the poor but how to do so—"the way in which this produce shall be taken from those who create it, and given to those who cannot create it" (3). She saw the public's options as, on the one hand, a system of cooperating public institutions and private charitable organizations and, on the other, unorganized private almsgiving. She urged the former essentially on the ground that tax-supported custodial and quasi-custodial institutions (workhouses, asylums, orphanages) were essential to a system that helped only the truly needy, discouraged the unworthy, and trained or rehabilitated the able-bodied for disciplined lives of productive work (67–69, 70–83).

Lowell did recommend that public institutions answer to "volunteer visitors" who would "represent the people at large" and "supply the precious element of human sympathy and tender personal interest which must often be lacking where the care of dependence is a business and the common every-day work the means of livelihood of over-taxed officials" (84). She also regarded charity a virtue and conceived it to describe only volunteer and therefore private efforts to help "the degraded" (84, 87–89). But a voluntary act of giving was, in her view, not necessarily an act of charity. To be an act of charity it must also have actually *benefited* the recipient by some objective test. And, she maintained, "indiscriminate [private] almsgiving" together with "systematic dole giving" (like most outdoor public relief) harmed the poor by making them dependent, falsely raising their expectations of adequate support, making them objects of resentment, and, above all, destroying their character (89–92).

Lowell believed that real help for the poor, at least in large urban areas (see 97–100), demanded an attitude, skills, and other resources possessed less by ordinary men and women than by social-service professionals—a willingness to deal "*radically*" with the causes of poverty in individual cases, even if "painful as plucking out an eye or cutting off a limb" (e.g., breaking up families of "drunkards"), and the knowledge and other resources for helping the poor free "their brains . . . from ignorance, their hands . . . from . . . incompetence, and their souls . . . from . . . sin" (94, 96, 105–6). Appealing to what she treated as an empirical fact of human nature drawn from such sources as the history

of the Irish Poor Laws, Lowell held that the natural sympathy of ordinary men and women was no match for the wiles of "unworthy beg-
gars." In a statement that suggests the social origin of property and a
social conception of liberty, she described the indiscriminate transfer
of property from one person to the next as a harmful tax on a public
resource—"a decided tax on industry, which would be increased almost indefinitely, were there no public and systematized means of relieving the poor" (3–4).

By conceiving private charity as the distribution of a public resource,
Lowell blurred the line between public and private. She was to do so
again when outlining the institutional makeup of effective charity.
Urging a system that combined public relief with organized and partially tax-supported private charity, she insisted on a measure of public
involvement in private charity. Volunteers and the concerned public
generally made a "great mistake," she said, when assuming "an attitude of antagonism toward the officials in public institutions . . . for
the amount of unselfishness and devotion . . . among those who spend
their lives in the distasteful ministry to ungrateful and degraded pau-
pers[,] insane and sick, can scarcely be imagined." To maintain standards and counter tendencies "to slackness . . . and even more serious
abuses," private charitable institutions "need regular and severe official inspection" by "persons who know what they are talking about."
Volunteers who care for "dependents of any class" must not forget that
"[i]t is not their own private affair whether those . . . under their protection are well or ill cared for; it is a public concern and good care
should be insured by public inspection" (84–85).

Lowell thus held the amelioration of poverty a clear public responsibility, and this despite her view, later to change,[25] that the causes of
poverty lay largely, though not exclusively, in the character of the
poor.[26] Perhaps most significantly for Currie's view of late-nineteenth-
century thought on the subject, Lowell did not view the problem of
poverty from the one-dimensional perspective of rational maximizers
contracting for the benefits of a mere nightwatchman state. She wrote
as one endowed with natural sympathy for others and as a citizen
eager to further the moral and material well-being of her community.
Her opposition to most forms of almsgiving and outdoor relief was a
fact-based and therefore contingent position that implied no general

---

[25] See Katz, *In the Shadow of the Poorhouse*, 71, 83.

[26] See Lowell, *Public Relief and Private Charity*, 107–8. In *Tragedy of American Compassion*,
at 79, Olasky suggests that Lowell generally opposed public aid, as distinguished from
private charity. If Olasky intends this suggestion, he cites no evidence for it, and none
can be found in Lowell's book.

or ideological opposition to either public or private efforts to help the poor. In her view: "The great point to be considered is what is possible. Could all men be made comfortable and happy by a charity so extended that it would amount to an equal division of the wealth of any given community, I should welcome the measure with my whole heart; but it has been proved, and surely it scarcely needed proving, that no amount of money scattered among people who are without character and virtue, will insure even physical comfort" (91–92).

Katz calls the system urged by Lowell and other theorists of scientific charity "organized charity" and their movement the "charity organization movement." As we have seen, this movement sought to replace public outdoor relief and indiscriminate private almsgiving with quasi-public, centrally directed confederations of private organizations ("charity organization societies") that substituted counseling for most material relief and reserved public custodial institutions for children, the disabled, and the aged.[27] This movement emerged in the 1870s and "spread from larger to smaller cities and from North to South" (86). It succumbed to the depression of 1893. With as much as 19 percent of the labor force out of work nationwide—Katz reports 35 percent in New York, 25 percent in Pennsylvania, and 43 percent in Michigan—and relief agencies swamped by "vastly increased demands for help," business leaders, politicians, and social-service professionals were forced to abandon or compromise their old assumptions about the causes of idleness (151–55). With "[e]ven conservatives" forced "to admit the structural roots of unemployment," says Katz, most observers now believed that "only government had the resources and authority to alleviate the misery endemic to modern industrial civilization" (154–55).

This awakening brought waves of municipal, administrative, and welfare reform to urban America. In the larger cities, welfare reform included professionally run and centralized boards or departments of public welfare. These agencies collected data on the living and working conditions of the poor and coordinated programs from cash assistance, housing, and legal aid to employment agencies, public works projects, and vacant-lot gardening. Funded only partly by city governments, these departments received "generous support" from business and private foundations. Katz notes that business support was due partly to the theory that effective departments of public welfare could ameliorate conditions favoring revolutionary socialism, a fear of the age (159–60). Yet public spending on the poor rose dramatically if unevenly. Dropping 8 percent from 1904 to 1912, public spending rose 79 percent from 1912 to 1930, and on the eve of the Great Depression most

[27] Katz, *In the Shadow of the Poorhouse*, 68–83.

cities were spending three times more than private agencies on out-door relief (159).

As Katz describes the period within which scientific charity "moved from the vanguard to the backwater of social policy," municipal governments continued to perform their long-recognized function of poor relief even as they experimented with a theory (i.e., scientific charity) that sought to end part of their immediate operational role. And the failure of that theory found these governments standing by to expand their involvement in cooperation with business and private charity. This general picture hardly conforms to the nightwatchman model of Currie's account.

This is not to say that by the late 1920s a social democratic wave had swept the country. Katz reports that for all the reforms and expansions of public relief in the first two decades of the twentieth century, "fictive boundaries between public and private" influenced public thinking on welfare policy and left governments willing "to intervene in economic decision" only as a "last resort." Katz attributes chronic underfunding of programs and the eventual failure of many welfare initiatives partly to this attitude (150–51). But his description of the situation finds "pieties of economic liberalism" coexisting with a social attitude that took public poor relief for granted, spawned the settlement movement, and made an activist like Jane Addams "the most admired American woman, often . . . the most admired American" in "every early-twentieth-century public opinion poll before World War I" (150, 167).

If Katz is right—if there in fact was such a tension between free-market ideology and the actual functions of government or between different beliefs about the role of government—that would suffice to refute Currie's claim that any finding of constitutional responsibility for poor relief would be "ahistorical." Beliefs and practices coexisting in tension would make for a mixed historical record, and a moral argument would be needed to exclude any part of the mixture from a normative constitutional judgment. Currie would have to contend that we ought to take our bearings from the free-market part of a mixed historical experience for one or both of two reasons: either because a free-market interpretation would put our history in its most attractive light morally or because such an interpretation would reinforce a tradition that best advances the general welfare. Currie argues for neither conclusion, nor could he do so without lapsing into a welfarist argument of some sort. If he defends a free-market account on some moral theory that separates moral rightness from the general welfare, he has first to connect moral rightness to the free market and then find a reason for preferring moral rightness to well-being in any and all conflicts between the two. If found, this reason would make Currie's argument a welfarist argument, for he would be arguing that it is better to be morally right than well-off in some way that conflicts with moral rectitude. Such an argument would conceive well-being as some austerely moral well-being; its ground might be Kant's proposal that the only unqualified good is a will disposed to act morally.[28]

Much the same holds for a free-market interpretation of American history *on the ground that* the free market best serves the general welfare: such an argument renders free-market tenets the contingent premises of a welfarist argument. The truth of any such premises would depend on the truth of philosophic and scientific arguments about what the public's well-being is and how best to approach it under foreseeable conditions. By advancing these tenets as arguments, not postulates, the free-marketeer (like anyone worth listening to) would implicitly assure his audience of his greater interest in the truth about the general welfare (what and how) than in his version of it, which he would then submit to moral and nonmoral evidence and argumentation. I shall have more to say about what the presuppositions of all such arguments imply for the welfare debate.

What is clear at this point is that the early history of state provision for the poor in America precludes Currie's categorical exclusion of "welfare" provision from the nation's founding principles. The relevant history is mixed at best, and Currie offers no normative argument for reading the historical record his way. A reading different from Currie's is suggested by the pointlessness of establishing a government for the sole purpose of limiting it, the goods envisioned by the Constitution's enumeration of substantive powers, Currie's own account of the origin of the Fourteenth Amendment, and Currie's own hedge against the ultimate implication of his position on "welfare" (no duty to police). Combine these considerations with the Constitution's institutional provisions and the Bill of Rights, and the Constitution emerges as more than a charter of negative liberties. It appears now as a charter for institutions organized and empowered to achieve social benefits, albeit in a manner consistent with individual rights.

WELFARE AND THE FRAMERS

Two remaining historical-textual objections confront positive constitutionalism, both linked more tightly than the considerations just canvassed to the specifics of the Constitution of 1789. Practices in the states

---

[28] I do not know how Currie would square such a view with the Constitution's history or the Constitution's Preamble, which envisions a government that works both for justice and for the general welfare. For a discussion of Kant's proposition, see Bruce Aune, *Kant's Theory of Morals* (Princeton, N.J.: Princeton University Press, 1979), 3–9.

before the Revolution and after the founding aside, one might say, the only relevant considerations are, first, the intentions of the framers and, second, the specific terms of *their* constitution. Terrance Sandalow takes this position when criticizing Lawrence Sager's argument for what I am calling a benefits model of the Constitution.[29]

"The concern of the founding generation was not that government would fail to act affirmatively to secure individual welfare," says Sandalow, "but that its powers would be employed oppressively" (446). To the negative end of preventing oppression the founders dedicated "restrictions on the exercise of power" and "more profoundly . . . structural provisions" like "[p]olitical accountability, federalism, the separation of powers, and institutional checks upon . . . power." The premise of these structural provisions was that "government is not a source of liberty, but a threat to it." "As a consequence," Sandalow continues, constitutional rights and structures were intended as limits on power, and the "powers of government were stated only permissively, as authorizations, not obligations" (464–65).

Sandalow acknowledges that "our [current] understanding of the Constitution has long since—and for good reason—overleapt those [original] boundaries." Yet he also holds that constitutional meaning has evolved "within channels whose starting point is the [constitutional] text and the ideas that animated it." Because "[t]he course of constitutional development has proceeded along the path set by the framers," he concludes, "we simply do not have a conceptual framework within which to address claims of affirmative governmental obligation. Neither the text nor an evolving constitutional tradition provides concepts or even a language that would guide [such a] discussion" (464–65).

Sandalow's point about a "conceptual framework" might be saved if it were scaled back to describe the current state of constitutional thought in America. Mainstream constitutional commentary is not preoccupied with such questions as the constitutionality of the Welfare Reform Act (officially the Personal Responsibility Act) of 1996, an act in which Congress seemed to disclaim a federal responsibility to provide for the material well-being of the nation's dependent children. Negative constitutionalism and the court-centeredness of most constitutional scholarship explain the paucity of debate on this issue. Legal academe tends to assume that the Constitution does not promise any benefits that courts cannot order Congress to provide in direct ways. But this assumption is false. Courts cannot order Congress to pass and appropriate funds for enforcing laws against slavery. Yet this fact

---

[29] See Sager, "Justice in Plain Clothes"; see also Sandalow, "Social Justice and Fundamental Law."

hardly justifies concluding that the Thirteenth Amendment does not (really) outlaw slavery or guarantee a state of civil freedom. A similar argument applies to the president's duty to defend against foreign invasions or Congress's duties to conduct the decennial census and to establish and fund a system of national courts: Courts cannot compel performance of these duties either, but few doubt that these duties enjoy constitutional status.

The question is how far examples like this will take us and whether they will take us as far as public aid for dependent children. Contending for a view of the Constitution that will take us at least that far, this book joins the works of other writers, like Sager and, before him, Michelman and Black. The established concerns of constitutional scholarship cannot refute these arguments by limiting what constitutional scholars can talk about. The question is not whether the current establishment acknowledges a framework for conducting the welfare debate in constitutional terms. The question is whether such a framework is available for establishment, whether that framework has constitutional provenance, and whether the scholarly community should adopt it.

As for Sandalow's understanding of the framers, the same understanding is evident in Currie's defense of *DeShaney*; it seems to be the established understanding. Not much more can be said for it, however. I cannot say in an unqualified way that both writers are flat wrong about "the framers" without knowing precisely to whom they refer, a question Walter Murphy has shown easier to ask than to answer.[30] But I do say both are flat wrong if the framers are fairly represented by the work with which "the framers" are most widely associated. That work, of course, is *The Federalist*. Here I summarize what I have written elsewhere, referring the reader to the same work for the reasons I sometimes prefer to speak of "Publius" rather than Hamilton, Madison, and Jay.[31] And perhaps it is not inappropriate for me to add here that I owe what readers will see as a "big-government" and "progressive" understanding of *The Federalist*, and therewith "the framers" and "the founding," principally to the works of three writers now generally regarded as ideological conservatives: Martin Diamond, Herbert Storing, and Walter Berns.[32]

---

[30] For the many problems connected to the question of just who the framers were, see Walter F. Murphy, "Constitutional Interpretation: The Art of the Historian, Magician, or Statesman?" *Yale Law Journal* 87 (1978): 1752–71.

[31] Barber, *Constitution of Judicial Power*, chap. 2.

[32] See Walter Berns, "The Meaning of the Tenth Amendment," in Robert Goldwin, ed., *A Nation of States* (Chicago: Rand McNally, 1963), 126–48; Herbert J. Storing, "The Problem of Big Government," in Goldwin, ed., *A Nation of States* 65–87; Storing, *What the Anti-Feder-*

Pace Sandalow on both framers' intentions and conceptual framework, Publius's argument in *The Federalist* generally reflects the instrumentalist or ends-oriented language and logic of the Constitution's
Preamble. Publius's main concern is the substantive *ends* or *purposes* of
government—the substantive benefits that good government can facilitate. The benefits he mentions range from particulars like a discharge
of the Revolutionary War debt and passage for American shipping on
the Mississippi (4:20; 7:41) to the comprehensive end of government,
which he describes variously as "the solid happiness of the people,"
"the real welfare of the great body of the people" (45:309) "Justice"
(51:347), and "the PUBLIC GOOD" (71:481–82). He thus treats institutions
like federalism and the separation of powers as means to the ends of
government, means an enlightened people would abandon should
they fail to achieve their purposes (45:308–9; 47:327, 331; 51:350–53).
No less applies to "the plan of the [Philadelphia] Convention" and "the
Union itself" (45:308–9). No less applies even to popular government
or democracy, a form of government he cannot recommend unless it
can "secure the public good, and private rights," avoid "the disorders
of [ancient] republics," and most generally approach "Justice," "the
end of [both] government [and] civil society," an end which "ever has
been, and ever will be pursued, until it be obtained, or until liberty be
lost in the pursuit" (10:61; 9:51; 51:352).

To secure the ends of government Publius proposes a strategy that
seeks, first, to prevent the tyranny of any institution or part of the community over others (10:63–64; 51:347–52) and, second, to provide the
"energy" government needs to enforce the laws (15:93, 95–96), ameliorate social problems (22.140–42), and prevent "the abuses of liberty,"
which are more "to be apprehended by the United States" than "the
abuses of power" (63:428–29). His substrategies for preventing tyranny
include the separation of powers described in *Federalist* No. 51 and the
large number of economic and religious groups described in *Federalist*
No. 10. His hopes for energetic government lie chiefly with the initiatives of a strong executive, especially in times of crisis and legislative
deadlock (22:140–41; 70:471–72; 71:481–83).

Publius's overriding concern for the ends of government brings him
to an understanding of governmental powers that differs from Sandalow's. Popularly granted powers are taken by Publius to imply not
mere authorizations but a fiduciary duty to pursue the ends for which
the powers were granted in the first place (23:146–49; 45:308–9; 71:482–
83). This positive outlook on governmental powers in turn moves

---

alists Were For, chap. 5; Martin Diamond, "The Federalist," in Leo Strauss and Joseph Crop-
sey, eds., *History of Political Philosophy* (Chicago: Rand McNally, 1972), 631–51.

Publius to affirm an ends-oriented approach to legal interpretation that is "dictated by plain reason as well as founded on legal axioms": that parts of a legal charge or authorization should be "made to conspire to some common end," and where "several parts cannot be made to coincide, the less important should give way to the more important . . . the means . . . sacrificed to the end, rather than the end to the means" (40:259–60).

Sandalow's focus on the means in a way that ignores the ends causes him to distort the nature of the means. No longer visible to Sandalow as aspects of a fiduciary trust, the powers of government are mere authorizations to be exercised or not, as officials might wish. Unconcerned with the substantive ends of government, Sandalow takes no notice of the framers' provision of the "energy" government needs to pursue substantive ends. Checks and balances thus constitute a mechanism for preventing bad things, not enabling good things. Sandalow seems unaware that Publius's specific theory of checks and balances is explicitly designed to weaken the Congress and strengthen the presidency as an independent agent of power (51:530). This independence for the executive proves later in Publius's account to be a leading condition for "energy in government"—chiefly through "energy in the executive" (70:471–72). The system of checks and balances thus empowers what Publius puts forth as the most *responsible* part of the government, with "responsibility" conceived as including not only accountability to the electorate but also, and more important, a concern for the public's true "interests," as opposed to its mere "inclinations." As Publius describes it, a fully responsible government performs an educative function by reconciling the public *to* its true interests (63:423–24; 70:471–72; 71:481–83).

Sandalow also overlooks Publius's description of checks and balances as "a policy of supplying by opposite and rival interests, the defect of better motives" (51:349). To understand the system as Publius understood it, one would have to account for it in terms of these better motives and the affirmative ends that inform them, as formulated, for example, in the Preamble: justice, the general welfare, domestic tranquility, the blessings of liberty (not unqualified liberty), and so forth. Sandalow's understanding will not do. It leaves us wondering why a people would undertake the great exertions needed to overthrow one old government and disestablish another, set up a new one, and give it powers to be exercised—not as duties, in the true interests of the people, but solely as the government might wish. Sandalow develops his position by criticizing Sager's view that government has affirmative constitutional duties beyond those that courts are competent to enforce.[33] Sager's view makes more practical sense; it is also far more consonant with the constitutional theory of *The Federalist*, and it reconciles the Constitution to what William J. Novak shows was the dominant conception of government at the state and municipal levels in America from the constitutional period until the late nineteenth century: "governance committed to the pursuit of the people's welfare and happiness in a well-ordered society and polity."[34]

[33] Sager, "Justice in Plain Clothes," 420–25.

[34] William J. Novak, *The People's Welfare: Law and Regulation in Nineteenth-Century America* (Chapel Hill: University of North Carolina Press, 1996), 2.

Chapter Three

NEGATIVE CONSTITUTIONALISM AND
UNWANTED CONSEQUENCES

Does a benefits model of the Constitution risk unwanted social consequences—consequences that negative constitutionalism can avoid? Arguments to this effect overlap both the historical arguments for the
negative constitution discussed in the last chapter and the philosophic
arguments to be discussed in the next chapter. In taking up the arguments from unwanted consequences, I do not pretend to predict the
future, and I concede that it is possible for the *rhetoric* of positive constitutionalism to make things worse for the *cause* of positive constitutionalism, which must be defined in terms of its motivating *end*: the
nation's well-being.[1] I argue here only that one cannot predict unhappy
consequences from the logic of positive constitutionalism, for that logic
promises no more or less than a good effort, as distinguished from
good results. And though I cannot prove it, I believe, and I doubt many
will deny, that a different opinion in *DeShaney* would have carried less
risk of Soviet-style totalitarianism than the risk that now comes with
DeShaney: governmental indifference to preventable suffering.

The Slippery Slope in General

Exponents of the negative-liberties model seem to fear that a slippery
slope connects the duty to provide the least that well-being requires,
like police protection, to the most for which egalitarian altruism can
reasonably wish, like a good education and a decent job for every responsible and competent person. This fear, says Susan Bandes, "is perhaps the most tenacious barrier" to recognizing affirmative constitutional duties.[2] Fear of the slippery slope is fed by several motivations,
including a desire to avoid judicial value judgments, which, for some,
translate into judicial impositions on democracy, and skepticism about

---

[1] For an argument that judicially enforced "welfare rights" could make matters worse
for the poor, see Frank B. Cross, "The Error of Positive Rights," *University of California
Law Review* 48 (2001): 857, 915–20.

[2] Bandes, "The Negative Constitution," 2230.

value judgments generally, which is widely (though falsely, as we shall see) thought to support (the value of) governmental neutrality associated with modern liberalism. Because a principled line separating police protection and at least some provision against market-induced insecurities is hard to find, and because negative constitutionalists assume (falsely, as we have seen) that state provision for market-induced insecurities uniquely requires coercing taxes from some people to benefit others, negative constitutionalists want to deny that government has any primary substantive duties at all. This position ignores the unavoidability of value choices in constitutional decision and the redistributive foundation of all governmental action, and it enables judges and others to favor the status quo without defending it. Bandes rightly suggests that the only responsible way to limit what constitutional government in America is obligated to pursue is not by denying any and all substantive obligations but by forming a theory of substantive constitutional ends and corresponding duties (2334–35).

Bandes's answer to the slippery-slope problem parallels Publius's response to a charge of the Anti-Federalists that the powers granted by the new constitution are too extensive for the liberties of the people. These powers, he says, are means to essential ends and must be adequate to the ends they envision—even if this means formally unlimited powers. Rather than complain about the powers of the new government, which are "not too extensive for the[ir] OBJECTS, . . . [i.e.,] our NATIONAL INTERESTS," critics should show that "the internal structure of the proposed government" renders it "unworthy of the confidence of the people" (23:147, 150–51). When it comes to constitutional powers, it thus seems that the slope is indeed slippery. But that cannot be an argument for denying powers that are needed, especially when the exercise of these powers can be limited in other ways.

Those who fear a slippery slope are unwilling to approve some results in a set defined by some principle out of disapproval of other results in the set. Disapproval of some results can move an observer to reject the principle that justifies the unwanted results and therewith other results that, standing alone, would be wanted. Ideological conservatives might reject an obligation to provide police protection because they strongly oppose poor support and because they see no principled way to provide one and deny the other. But aversion to particular results serves argument against a broader principle only when addressed to persons who share the speaker's aversion to the results in question. When I turned Currie's slope against him by emphasizing that the negative-liberties model implies no duty to provide police protection, I assumed readers who agree that no duty to police is indeed, as Currie himself eventually puts it, "unthinkable."

As the close contest over ratification of the Constitution indicates, slippery-slope arguments against governmental power can be successful with the general public. Its rhetorical power aside, however, the slippery-slope argument for the negative-liberties model ought to be a poor argument among constitutional theorists. The negative libertarian's fear of the slope assumes the existence of the slope. But that very assumption favors the benefits model. For the slope is nothing other than the absence of a principled reason for the selective relief of insecurities. No principled reason for ameliorating some insecurities but not others is precisely what constitutes the slope. An aversion to poor support without a principled reason for denying poor support while granting other benefits forces the negative libertarian to an untenable denial of a duty to provide any benefits, including police protection.

The slippery-slope argument is attractive to those whose expectation of bad results is stronger than their expectation of good results. It leaves them in a position that assumes the Constitution establishes a government to limit it. But such a constitution would be a pointless one, and in fact the Constitution not only limits government but also establishes a government and empowers it. It thus expresses both hopes for government and fears of government. Establishing a government when fear of bad results overpowers expectations of good results would be as incomprehensible as establishing a government solely for the sake of limiting it. When negative constitutionalists try to avoid the slippery slope, they replace a sensible constitution with a pointless one. Bandes's solution is better; it saves the Constitution as the rational and deliberate expression that ordinary Americans suppose it to be. Seen against the background of the kind of theory for which Bandes calls and whose possibility I defend in this book, the slippery-slope problem disappears. No one persuaded to any defensible theory of constitutional ends will deny that the Constitution obligates the national government to do what it legitimately can to facilitate the general welfare, even if that means facilitating only the private pursuit of happiness reasonably conceived.

DOES WELFARE CONSTITUTIONALISM UNDERMINE NEGATIVE LIBERTIES?

Another way to pursue the negative-liberty argument against a welfare model of the Constitution is to contrast the American Constitution with the constitutions of totalitarian states like the former Soviet Union and its communist allies.[3] Unlike constitutions that follow the Ameri-

---

[3] Steven G. Calabresi pursues this strategy against Robin West's proposal for an "aspirational constitution" that favors forward-looking legislative power over a court-cen-

can model, the argument goes, communist constitutions fuse public and private spheres, emphasize the duties and obligations (as distinguished from the negative liberties) of citizens, and list general aspirations in the form of positive rights (to education, health care, and retirement security, for example) to be secured through legislation, not judicial action.

This account of the differences between American- and Soviet-style constitutions appears as part of Cass Sunstein's analysis of problems facing Eastern European constitution makers in the early 1990s.[4] Sunstein advised the Eastern Europeans not to list affirmative substantive guarantees in their constitutions beyond protections (some negative, some positive) for property and contractual rights. Sunstein expressly tailored his advice for a socialist political culture trying to fortify itself for the painful transition to Western-style markets and democratic processes. In a line that reflects a famous passage in *Federalist* No. 10 (and that bespeaks a positive constitutionalism), Sunstein said constitutions "should be designed to work against precisely those aspects of a country's culture and tradition that are likely to cause harm through that country's ordinary political processes" (216). Because a socialist culture needs no constitutional reminder to serve the needs of its people, none is indicated—especially when constitutionally guaranteed welfare rights will cool the investor confidence needed for economic growth, a leading element of the people's welfare (206–7, 216–22).

But Sunstein has different advice for Americans, who "may be too focused on the functions of constitutions in courts [as sources of negative liberties] and insufficiently attentive to the cultural consequences of constitutional guarantees." In this country, says Sunstein, constitu-

---

tered regime that emphasizes limitations on legislative power. Calabresi argues generally that the trend of modern constitutionalism has been toward the negative model and that this model has not proved hostile to left-liberal or progressive policies. See Steven G. Calabresi, "Thayer's Clear Mistake," *Northwestern University Law Review* 88 (1993): 269; and Robin West, "The Aspirational Constitution," *Northwestern University Law Review,* 88:241 (1993).

Chief Justice Rehnquist hints at this strategy in *DeShaney* when denying that Wisconsin had a duty to protect Joshua arising from a "special relationship" between the state and persons, like convicts, held in custody by the state. With regard to such persons, he says, the Constitution does "impose[] upon the State affirmative duties of care and protection," for the state has deprived these persons of the liberty to care for themselves. But Joshua, he contends, was in his father's custody, not the state's; and "[w]hile the State may have been aware of the dangers that Joshua faced in the free world, it played no part in their creation, nor did it do anything to render him any more vulnerable to them" (489 U.S. 201).

[4] Cass R. Sunstein, *Free Markets and Social Justice* (New York: Oxford University Press, 1997), 205.

tion makers may rationally decide to list "positive rights . . . to encourage political attention to fundamental matters (such as shelter, subsistence, medical care, and environmental quality) and to insure that statutes are interpreted in light of a full range of appropriate social commitments" (214). The nation's political culture makes Sunstein confident that a constitutional right "to some forms of social assistance . . . could not possibly threaten the general belief in markets, solid property rights, and civil society" (215).

Sunstein's confidence is surely well-founded. The effect of my argument to this point is that the nation now has and always has had positive constitutions at both the state and national levels, for security, prosperity and other desiderata are the only things that can motivate the establishment of popular constitutions. These goods in fact did motivate our constitution makers (or so they said and, for political reasons, had to say), and our governments with government generally, as Walzer observes, have always claimed to pursue the well-being of their populations. Yet in the face of these realities, most academic opinion and the Supreme Court classify the Constitution as a charter of negative liberties, and the apparent motivation for doing so is to protect a market and a civil society naively believed to enjoy some meaningful independence from law-laden and therefore state-created or state-maintained goods, options, and infrastructures. The very currency of this negative constitutionalism, illusory though it be, is ample evidence for Sunstein's confidence in behalf of market and society as we know it.

Nevertheless, positive constitutionalists have reasons to feel that their position could eventually compromise negative liberties and other points of difference, real and imagined, between American- and Soviet-style constitutions. Because the positive constitution would charge elected legislators with affirmative constitutional duties, it would implicitly define the responsibilities of voters in related terms and thus presuppose citizenship that elevates the personal rewards of participation in praiseworthy political action over conflicting private goods. Taken to heart by influential people in academe, this positive view of the Constitution might gain a toehold in educated public opinion generally and then . . . who knows?

Such a transformation, improbable though it be, could weaken rights that function as exemptions from governmental power. By putting the Constitution on the side of goods facilitated largely through legislation, the positive view constitutionalizes the substance of appropriately directed legislation, not just the authority to enact legislation. Good examples would be the Sherman Act and the Civil Rights Act of 1964. Each was seen by its supporters as constitutional both with respect to Congress's authority to enact and with respect to substantive policy objectives, the former envisioning a competitive market whose structure and operation both reflected and provided the socioeconomic conditions for the theory of *Federalist* No. 10 and the latter redeeming the larger promises of the Thirteenth and Fourteenth Amendments. When constitutionally indifferent exercises of power conflict with constitutional rights, the Constitution favors rights. But when constitutionally *directed* power conflicts with constitutional rights, the Constitution seems to support both sides, thus compromising rights. The history of state-federal contests in American constitutional law illustrates this last situation. In *McCulloch v. Maryland* (1819), John Marshall conceived authorized congressional action in terms of constitutional ends and declared conflicting state policies unconstitutional merely by virtue of the conflict, rejecting a not unreasonable claim of states' rights under the Tenth Amendment.[5] Until they were abandoned by the Rehnquist Court, the policies of affirmative action and racially integrated schools illustrated the same: policy makers pursued racial justice as a constitutional end notwithstanding the perceived disadvantage of whites claiming freedoms of choice and association and a right against reverse discrimination.

Yet these very examples suggest a strategy for curing the risks they illustrate: soften the apparent clash between negative liberties and affirmative constitutional ends by narrowing the scope of the liberties. With John Marshall one might say that the states have no right to exercise their legislative power in ways that conflict with constitutionally directed national power. With Justice William Brennan one could say that even a constitutional state practice is no barrier to well-considered congressional attempts to combat historical racial injustices.[6] Some positive constitutionalists (not a homogeneous lot regarding substantive matters) will approve Justice Sandra Day O'Connor's compromising a woman's freedom of choice to accommodate what they see as a state's affirmative duty to protect prenatal life,[7] or Justice Antonin Scalia's willingness to compromise exercises of religious freedom when they conflict with ends traditionally served by the criminal law.[8] An alternative to denying or paring down rights in conflict with constitutional ends is to build strong rights into one's conception of constitutional ends. Such was Justice Robert H. Jackson's method when denying in the second flag-salute case that "national unity" could constitutionally mean the "[c]ompulsory unification . . . of the grave-

---

[5] 4 Wheat. 316 (1819).

[6] *Katzenbach v. Morgan*, 384 U.S. 641 (1966).

[7] *Planned Parenthood v. Casey*, 505 U.S. 833 (1992).

[8] *Employment Division v. Smith*, 494 U.S. 872 (1990).

yard," his symbol for the conformism he found implicit in forcing children to salute the flag.[9] Whether and how to compromise rights or conceive them as elements of constitutional ends will depend on contingencies and on one's conception of constitutional ends. Unavoidable in either case would be the need to justify one's conception of negative liberties in terms of some theory of constitutional ends, ends that include the general welfare.

The negative liberties in question here are constitutional rights—that is, constitutionally recognized immunities from constitutionally granted powers to pursue constitutionally authorized ends like national security and the general welfare. Arrangements between rights and powers of this sort do not have to make sense, and it may not be immediately evident that the Constitution's arrangement does. Publius contends in *Federalist* No. 23 that in fact it does not make sense to limit national powers granted for needed ends. Powers "essential to . . . the common defence, " he says, "ought to exist without limitation: *Because it is impossible to foresee or define the extent and variety of national exigencies, or the corresponding extent & variety of the means which may be necessary to satisfy them*" (23:147, his emphasis). This is not a hedge for military emergencies on Publius's part, for later in the same paper he applies this principle "to commerce, and to every other matter" within the jurisdiction of the proposed government (23:149). So, if limitations on admittedly needed powers are to make sense, some assumptions must be made.

The first assumption concerns a rank ordering of apprehensions. The fear of government must not be greater than the fear of private power, in which fear liberal theory says the need for government originates. Establishing a government would be irrational where government is feared as much as or more than the private power government is to suppress and displace. For this reason limiting needed powers must come to terms with Publius's statement that where people need government because men are not angels, and where people need controls on government because angels do not govern men, framers of government "must first enable the government to controul the governed; and in the next place oblige it to controul itself" (51:349). To make sense of limits on admittedly needed powers, the limitations must therefore be reconciled *to* the powers; constitutional rights must be reconciled *to* constitutional ends. This reconciliation can be sought by conceiving constitutional limitations as either instruments or constituents of constitutional ends, the ends envisioned by constitutional powers. The right to criticize the government's defense policies may thus be seen

---

[9] *West Virginia v. Barnette*, 319 U.S. 624 (1943).

as integral to any hope for national security, national security itself, as opposed to the government's conception of national security, which may be false and will be false sooner or later, assuming the human fallibility that deliberately established constitutions manifestly assume. Additionally, the capacity for reasoned self-direction, and thus (reasonably limited) rights of privacy, conscience, and property in a society of mutually accountable persons, may be seen both as presupposed by the right to criticize and as an element of the general welfare to which the Constitution is committed. This same praiseworthy capacity and related virtues may be seen as the point of constitutional structures designed to force self-serving parties into patterns of deliberative bargaining that approximate defensible versions of the public interest—structures that "supply[] by opposite and rival interests, the defect of better motives," as Publius puts it (51:349), and whose reflection of constitutional aspirations must depend to some extent on whether they work as Publius supposes.

I say more about this manner of conceiving constitutional rights and structural limitations on power at several points in the pages that follow, especially when offering a substantive theory of the general welfare in chapter 5. But no particular theory of limitations on power is as important for the purposes of this book as the general strategy of reconciling rights and other limits *to* the pursuit of public purposes and cabining those (like unrestricted gun ownership and liberty to contract) that cannot be so construed. The strategy is now a familiar one in constitutional theory and allied fields. Many writers have defended judicial independence, a structural limitation on power, as a practice that, at its ideal best, reflects a model of self-critical, open-minded, and principled action that (in Socratic fashion) both serves and improves upon its sources of authority.[10] The same can apply to rights. Holmes and Sunstein reject as "obviously too simple" any strong notion of rights "as trumps" that "the solitary individual raises against the community in which he or she was born and bred." And this because "rights are interests on which we, as a community, have bestowed special protection, usually because they touch upon 'the public interest'—

---

[10] See Ronald Dworkin, *A Matter of Principle* (Cambridge: Harvard University Press, 1985), 69–71; Frank Michelman, "The Supreme Court, 1985 Term—Foreword: Traces of Self-Government," *Harvard Law Review* 100 (1986): 4–77; Stephen G. Salkever," 'Lopp'd and Bound': How Liberal Theory Obscures the Good of Liberal Practice," in R. Bruce Douglass, Gerald M. Mara, and Henry S. Richardson, eds., *Liberalism and the Good* (New York: Routledge, 1990), 178–83; James Boyd White, *When Words Lose Their Meaning: Constitutions and Reconstitution of Language and Community* (Chicago: University of Chicago Press, 1984), 269–70; Lawrence G. Sager, "The Incorrigible Constitution," *New York University Law Review* 65 (1990): 933–36, 958–61.

that is, because they involve either the interests of the collectivity as a whole or the fair treatment of various members of the community. By recognizing, protecting, and financing rights, the collectivity fosters what are widely construed to be the deeper interests of its members."[11]

Holmes and Sunstein illustrate this arrangement by construing private property, perhaps the paradigmatic liberal right, much the way Aristotle does: as a social institution created and maintained in ways that encourage individuals to improve their property for the "social purposes" of enhancing "a nation's real estate and capital stock."[12] This view of property rights, though morally based, is well insulated from charges of ahistoricity by the findings of William Novak and other historians. Citing classical and early American usage governing the word "economy," eighteenth-century authorities like Vattel and Blackstone, and the pervasive regulatory practices of the American states from the eighteenth century to the last third of the nineteenth century, Novak finds that "[l]aw and state were not simply instrumentalities" of some autonomous market emerging by an "invisible, self-regulating law of supply and demand." Law and state were rather "the central creators of . . . economy as a special sphere of social activity, a sphere distinctly cognizable as an object of governance" and "only interpretable through the mass" of regulatory activity for pursuing "*salus populi*, the people's welfare."[13] Publius presupposes some such understanding when he says that the "principal task of modern Legislation" is the regulation of conflicting property interests (10:59). This famous statement is a one-liner; Publius does not explain or justify it. He shows in this way that he expects an audience that does not view regulation of the economy as governmental "interference" in some sphere of social activity presumptively beyond government's competence and legitimate concern.

But what about *liberty*? Negative constitutionalism may offer better protection for liberty, and positive constitutionalism may undermine liberty, at least eventually. This seems to be the inadvertent suggestion of Stephen Macedo in an important recent book whose principal views of liberal constitutionalism (as dependent on and empowered to foster liberal attitudes through public education as a form of state welfare) are consonant with the positive constitutionalism defended here. In a passage I find inconsistent with his larger purposes, Macedo proposes that "the foremost liberal virtues" are "the basic liberties . . . familiar from bills of rights: freedom of religious practice, rights of association

---

[11] Holmes and Sunstein, *The Cost of Rights*, 115–16.
[12] Ibid.; see also Aristotle's *Politics*, 1263a.
[13] Novak, *The People's Welfare*, 86–88, and works cited at 285 n. 9.

... freedom to express your opinion, to travel," and so on. "Closely connected with these basic liberties," he adds, "are the familiar defensive mechanisms designed to check abuses of power and safeguard basic individual liberties against the encroachments of government: constitutional devices ... [like] the separation of powers, legislative bicameralism, and the rule of law." His summary term for this cluster of immunities and structures is *"negative constitutionalism,"* a conception of government in which "respect " for "basic liberties" is "politically paramount." From this paramountcy it follows for Macedo that (quoting Isaiah Berlin) "'participation in self-government is, like justice, a basic requirement, and an end in itself.'"[14]

In this peripheral part of Macedo's larger argument, he seems to conflate the ends of government with negative liberties. To see why this would be a mistake, consider the relationship between speech and the negative liberty to speak without governmental interference or repercussions. Because speech is something we can have a right *to*, it can be distinguished from the right. Speech, as distinguished from a negative freedom of speech in the Bill of Rights, is thus an activity, a practice, or a faculty. Somewhat similarly, liberty and privacy, as distinguished from negative rights to same, are states of being. And self-government itself (not rights thereto) is a faculty or a practice or a state of being. Speech, liberty, and privacy can be ends of government if conceived as faculties, practices, and states of being, for it makes sense to establish a government to promote, facilitate, or protect faculties, practices, and states of being. But it makes no sense to establish a government for the purpose of limiting the government, and negative constitutional liberties are, in strictness, no more than limits on government. Nor does it make sense to establish a government when either aversion to, or expectation of, governmental harms is stronger than the attraction to, or expectation of, governmental benefits. For these reasons, negative liberties cannot function as constitutional ends, and negative liberties cannot be normatively paramount to constitutional ends.

A related reason negative liberties cannot be paramount to constitutional ends is that a right draws its value from the value of the right's content. No one values limiting government per se; limiting government's power over speech and privacy is valuable only to the extent that speech and privacy are valuable. And since a thing that has no value in itself cannot be an end in itself, a negative liberty cannot be an end in itself. Negative rights draw no value even from their protec-

[14] Stephen Macedo, *Diversity and Distrust: Civic Education in a Multicultural Democracy* (Cambridge: Harvard University Press, 1999), 8–9, his emphasis. Macedo quotes from Berlin, "Two Concepts of Liberty," in Berlin, *Four Essays on Liberty*, 310–11.

tion of speech and privacy. For negative rights do not actually protect these things; they are protected not by rights but by governmental power. Thus, as Holmes and Sunstein observe, the protection of things like speech from abridgment by agents of the state depends, minimally, on the willingness and the power of the state to tax and spend for the institutions needed to declare and remedy violations of negative liberties. The same point appears in Storing's defense of the Federalists' early opposition to a bill of rights. Emphasis on a bill of rights, they feared—and the currency of negative constitutionalism now justifies this fear—"might weaken *government*, which," said Storing, "is the first protection of rights."[15] It is in light of this dependence of negative liberties on affirmative exertions of governmental power that Holmes and Sunstein can legitimately doubt the integrity of the very concept of negative liberties.[16]

Negative constitutional liberties do not even provide an adequate legal basis for state protection of valuable things like speech and privacy. Negative liberties can provide a basis for protecting faculties and practices like speech and states of being like liberty, but only from government. When it comes to *private* assaults on speech, liberty, and the rest, negative constitutional liberties do little or nothing. The inadequacy of negative liberties can readily be seen by considering the case of slavery. Had the Thirteenth Amendment marked no more than exemption from state power, it would have abolished property in human beings only when title was held by states, not by private parties. Few would have described the resulting state of affairs in terms of "liberty." The liberty envisioned depended and still depends on the application of the Thirteenth Amendment to private parties as well as government, and on the passage and subsequent enforcement of, and public support for, appropriate acts of Congress. These acts begin with the Civil Rights Act of 1866, passed by Congress under the enforcement provision of the Thirteenth Amendment partly in response to the failure of the southern states to redress private violence against former slaves.

A negative libertarian is unlikely to answer this argument with the claim that private titles to slaves would amount to state action because state action is needed to enforce the private titles. I would certainly agree that a state that permits slavery actively protects slavery, if only by enforcing the state's civil and criminal laws against those whose opposition to slavery cannot await lawful changes in legal arrangements that permit slavery. The same holds for abortion: Permitting it is tantamount to protecting it by enforcing the criminal and civil laws

---

[15] Storing, *What the Anti-Federalists Were For*, 69, his emphasis.
[16] Holmes and Sunstein, *The Cost of Rights*, 39–43.

against those who cannot stop it save by unlawful or tortious behavior. This manner of active and fairly direct state support for whatever is not expressly prohibited by law puts the liberal state behind whatever it permits and belies much of the distinction between state and private action. The only truly private action is action that is either unknown by the public or illegal. But if a welfarist can accept all of this, a negative constitutionalist can accept none of it. He must construe state action narrowly lest a duty to restrain the state's encroachments on liberty be construed as a duty to protect liberty, which duty can elevate governmental power, even massively deadly power, over private power, as happened in the Civil War.

The same holds for speech, privacy, self-government, and similar goods. They make sense as ends of government. Their pursuit and protection demands governmental power; they cannot be secured by governmental inaction. Those who value liberty, speech, privacy, and the rest will therefore value power more than negative liberties. They will reject negative constitutionalism from an appreciation of Publius's statement that "the vigour of government is essential to the security of liberty; that, in the contemplation of a sound and well informed judgment, their interests can never be separated; and that a dangerous ambition more often lurks behind the specious mask of zeal for the rights of the people, than under the forbidding appearance of zeal for the firmness and efficiency of government" (1:5–6).

A Benefits Model and Liberalism's Private Sphere

Macedo himself eventually rejects negative constitutionalism. He describes his project initially as an attempt to restore a balance between a preoccupation with individual rights and the need for social attitudes and institutions that support political liberalism, which he defines at one point as centrally concerned with "personal liberty and the defense of basic individual rights."[17] Struck with the dependence of political liberalism on private attitudes and institutions, especially attitudes toward religion, Macedo argues that a liberal regime can legitimately and forthrightly foster liberal attitudes, accommodate religions friendly to political liberalism, and refuse accommodation to antiliberal religions. While he acknowledges the paradoxical nature of his position, and while he tries to agree with John Rawls that liberalism is essentially a set of *political* commitments, not concerned with matters of private morality and religious or deep cosmological faith, he recog-

---

[17] Macedo, *Diversity and Distrust*, x.

nizes that some private institutions, attitudes, and beliefs are actively antiliberal, *and* that "the health of our regime depends on its ability to turn people's deepest convictions—including their religious beliefs— in directions that are congruent with the ways of a liberal republic" (ix– x, 42–43, 166–74). He eventually calls this "fundamental constitutive project" a "basic task of positive constitutionalism" (157), and in summoning constitutional theorists to this task, he implicitly abandons negative constitutionalism.

Positive constitutionalists have but one honest response to the concern that their position threatens liberalism's "private sphere." They have to recognize with Macedo that separations of public and private spheres can be taken to untenable and self-defeating extremes. As indicated by recent judicial shifts in areas like school desegregation and affirmative action, as long demonstrated by political scientists,[18] and as Publius puts it in *Federalist* No. 84: the security of private rights, "whatever fine declarations may be inserted in any constitution, . . . must altogether depend on public opinion, and on the general spirit of the people and of the government" (84:580). This means a government that would secure rights that negative libertarians want secured must breach the private sphere at least to the point of (1) actively if indirectly encouraging liberal attitudes (e.g., through promoting economic opportunity and growth, taxing antiliberal elements along with other segments of the public to fund public schools from which racist and sectarian practices and instruction are excluded, other taxing and spending policies that foster liberal attitudes), and (2) discouraging, by uncompromising application of the civil and criminal law to conduct that they cause, sentiments that are too intensely antiliberal to permit living peacefully with liberal practices (regarding school prayer, for example, or abortion).

Breaching privacy to protect privacy seems paradoxical until one realizes, with Macedo, that attitudes that run to antiliberal extremes can destroy a regime of private rights. By emphasizing the duties of legislators who are elected by private citizens, positive constitutionalism does presuppose certain attitudes on the part of voters, taxpayers, potential military conscripts, and others who are expected to make different degrees and kinds of sacrifices for the common good. Positive constitutionalism also presupposes attitudes on the part of welfare clients, like a desire for self-sufficiency, that favor outcomes which attest "wel-

---

[18] Robert H. Dahl, "Decision Making in a Democracy: The Supreme Court as National Policy-Maker," *Journal of Public Law* 6 (1957): 293; Gerald N. Rosenberg, *The Hollow Hope* (Chicago: University of Chicago Press, 1991), 9–21.

fare's" contributions to the common good, outcomes like people employed in generally useful and "laudable pursuits." I return to these matters later in this book.

DOES A WELFARE CONSTITUTION REACH TOO HIGH?

Part of Sunstein's advice to the Eastern Europeans can apply to welfarist conceptions of constitutional possibilities in America: A list of guaranteed constitutional benefits like health care, education, housing, and employment invites disappointment with the Constitution when government fails to secure timely results of sufficient quality for sufficient numbers of people; and failure is always a prospect where goals are vague, costly, and dependent on both chance and the virtues of taxpayers, clients, and public managers. Better, therefore, to eschew positive constitutional duties and stick with judicially enforceable negative liberties.[19] This advice resonates with Publius's statement in *Federalist* No. 49 to the effect that constitution makers should avoid arrangements that remind the public of constitutional defects, for "the most rational government will not find it a superfluous advantage, to have the prejudices of the community on its side" (49:340). Yet positive constitutionalists can have mixed feelings about Sunstein's advice, as he himself does when indicating it may not apply with full force to Western constitutions. The advice seems sound because some degree of failure is guaranteed by the fact that constitutional ends can only be approached, not fully realized. Yet failure is a prospect for all constitutional provisions and arrangements, negative liberties included. Failure, moreover, is a prospect that constitutionalists must continually confront, even embrace, to remain constitutionalists.[20]

Constitutional aspirations like justice and the general welfare are merely approachable as long as one conceives them as they are conceived in ordinary political life: as real states of affairs that are objectively good. I defend a realist (or objectivist) conception of such goods in the next chapter, so I shall assume here that justice and the general welfare are or can be objective goods. If, then, the general welfare is a state of affairs whose properties are determined by its nature, as distinguished from mere opinions or conceptions of its nature, then any

---

[19] Sunstein, *Free Markets and Social Justice*, 213.

[20] I defend this proposition in Barber, *On What the Constitution Means*, chap. 3, esp. 59–61 and 151–52. See also John E. Finn, *Constitutions in Crisis: Political Violence and the Rule of Law* (New York: Oxford University Press, 1991), chap. 1, esp. 40–43.

given conception of the general welfare can be wrong, and progress toward knowledge of the real thing must proceed experimentally and dialectically and in a way that never quite closes the normative gap between opinion and knowledge. If progress is to occur, therefore, any given conception of well-being must be open to question, and any success must be seen as temporary and conditional. Where one conception prevails so completely that it is no longer criticized, no one can consciously accept its success, for perceiving a conception's (temporary and conditional) success comes from vindicating it against criticism, even if only hypothetical criticism. Disagreement and the prospect of failure are integral to America's constitutional understanding by virtue of the assumed reality of the things to which the nation aspires.

Sunstein's view that the Eastern Europeans should entrench negative rights, not positive rights, has to be qualified by his later insight regarding the cost of rights. The actual enjoyment even of negative rights comes only if legislatures and therefore taxpayers are willing to forgo other goods to pay for expensive judicial systems to vindicate claims against officials and to monitor prisons, police departments, and other tax-funded institutions. Sunstein thus sees the enforcement of any rights as a matter of public policy justified as a public good and pursued in large part by legislative and therefore ultimately public support. We have also seen that the enforcement of many traditional rights (speech, press, reasonable privacy of persons and property, etc.) should be seen as a constitutional end embraced within such preambulatory goods as justice and the general welfare. As a tax-funded public policy that pursues ends whose meanings are disputed and whose success depends on attitudes, persons, conditions, and institutions beyond judicial control, the enforcement of "negative liberties" is as amenable to failure as the attempt to provide any other positive good. If the prospect of failure argues against lists of positive guarantees, it argues against lists of negative liberties. And if failure is categorically more likely when government seeks goods other than negative liberties, then government is always more likely to do bad things than good. That would make establishing government an irrational act, which a constitutionalist as such cannot concede.

A better argument against lists of positive guarantees via either formal constitutional amendment or judicial construction is that any new list of positive rights would be both unnecessary and counterproductive. Proposing such a list might be interpreted as a concession to the negative-liberties view that the Constitution now promises no benefits. But the Preamble does promise the pursuit of justice, the general welfare, the blessings of liberty, and other goods; it does so by conceiving the body of the Constitution as an instrument of these goods. Article V makes the amendments part of this instrument by declaring them "part of this Constitution." As a matter of constitutional logic, therefore, the Constitution's so-called negative liberties are parts of an overarching welfarist scheme. The constitutional text thus supports the view of Holmes and Sunstein that enforcing rights is a matter of public policy justified as a public good. By its terms the Constitution is a charter of benefits. It was defended as a charter of benefits by *The Federalist*, as we have seen, and it makes sense interpreted no other way. Interpreting it as a charter of benefits could only proceed along the lines of Publius's "two rules of construction" set forth in *Federalist* No. 40 as "dictated by plain reason, as well as founded on legal axioms": allow the several parts of a legal expression meanings that "conspire to some common end"; and "where the several parts cannot be made to coincide, the less important part should give way to the more important part; the means should be sacrificed to the end, rather than the end to the means" (40:259–60). Taking the Preamble seriously and following Publius's commonsense rules would have led to a different opinion in *DeShaney* without anyone having to add anything to what is already in the Constitution.

The strongest reason to reject a further specification of benefits is the nature of the benefits sought. As I have emphasized, the Constitution promises (must be understood as promising) to promote *the general welfare*—the real thing—not some conception of the real thing, for any given conception could be wrong or incomplete (will be challenged as wrong or incomplete in a truly constitutional regime), especially as conditions change. So a specification of benefits may fall short of the general welfare or eventually even defeat it if policy makers limit themselves to that specification. For this reason positive constitutionalists can oppose constitutionalizing specific entitlements. Some positive constitutionalists may even have reservations about specifying a general right of responsible persons actually to enjoy "the minimum necessities of a decent life," for that right implies a duty that can fall to events and material conditions beyond government's control. These constitutionalists may seek, rather, the right to a government that acknowledges its duty to promote the well-being of all its people and that performs its duty as best it can in changing circumstances. The right in question would be a right not to success but to dutiful effort and progress relative to the community's resources. Constitutional failure would be chiefly a failure of will—chronic capture of government by persons who refuse to do their best in pursuit of constitutional ends.

The right to dutiful effort and relative progress need be neither alien nor toothless. Its elements are implicit in Lincoln's Special Message to Congress of July 4, 1861, a speech that justifies war—power in its clear-

est form—to preserve the Union, which Lincoln saw as a necessary
condition of all constitutional ends. In the speech Lincoln describes his
action against the rebellious states as an effort "guided by the Constitution" that seeks to "preserve the Government, that it may be administered for all, as it was administered by the men who made it." "Loyal
citizens," says Lincoln in welfarist fashion, "have the right to claim this
of their government, and the Government has no right to withhold or
neglect it."[21] He then describes the government as one "whose leading
object is to elevate the condition of men; to lift artificial weights from
all shoulders; to clear the paths of laudable pursuit for all; to afford all
an unfettered start and a fair chance in the race of life" (607). Lincoln
claims with pride that "the plain people understand and appreciate
this" (607), and that "[i]t may be affirmed, without extravagance, that
the free institutions we enjoy have developed the powers and improved the condition of our whole people beyond any example in the
world . . . [as attested by the size of the volunteer army and the] . . .
many single regiments whose members, one and another, possess full
practical knowledge of all the arts, sciences, professions, and whatever
else, whether useful or elegant, is known in the world" (606). The right
to a government that does its best made a big difference to the nation
under Lincoln, and had it been a prominent article of the Senate's constitutional faith during the appropriate confirmation hearings, it would
have meant a different opinion and perhaps a trial on the merits in
DeShaney.

Honoring an affirmative right to the conscientious and public-spirited use of legislative power would involve judicial protection for freedoms of conscience, speech, and political association, rights of political
participation, rights of property, and other rights that enable persons
to form and represent independent opinions about matters of public
concern.[22] Without the robust expression of such independent opinions,
the public has little knowledge of what or how the government is
doing. These rights are integral to, not competitive with, the pursuit of
public purposes. Positive constitutionalism needs the individual and
her private rights because seekers of goods presumed to be real have
reason to believe that they and the community can always be wrong
in both their conceptions of the goods and the means thereto and that
all should actively aspire to be right. This is no Soviet constitutionalism.

But an argument from the other side persists: The modern liberal
state has forsaken what some of its citizens earnestly see as among
the most fundamental of rights, like freedoms of racist association and

[21] Basler, *Lincoln: His Speeches and Writings*, 608.
[22] See Michelman, "Welfare Rights in a Constitutional Democracy," 675.

sectarian exercise,[23] and positive constitutionalism can easily make matters worse for these people. If the right to a government that does its best is to be enforced by the force behind such a government, namely, the electorate, then the object of positive constitutionalism can only be a virtuous electorate or some surrogate thereof, like a trusted and virtuous elite. And if positive constitutionalists seek the general welfare itself, the virtue in question would be a kind of self-critical and permissive liberalism that emphasizes truth over convention and authority, and values some degree of pluralism, toleration, and personal experimentation. This in itself would offend communities based on sectarian, hierarchical, and nonrational commitments like race, religiosity, and sexuality. The goal, moreover, of a public-spirited, open-minded, self-critical, and self-restraining electorate of continental proportions is too visionary for serious consideration. Publius makes the point in *Federalist* No. 49: "[A] nation of philosophers is as little to be expected as the philosophical race of kings wished for by Plato" (49:340). Only slightly less remote is the goal of a citizenry virtuous enough first to produce and then to trust an appropriately virtuous and engaged stratum of politicians, journalists, bureaucrats, educators, legal and public-health professionals, business leaders, and other opinion leaders.

Far more likely is a population whose real-life needs and limitations force it into decisions that fall far short of truths that are elusive in any case. Born of practical necessities, these decisions will interrupt endless philosophic striving and mark the limits of diversity and toleration.[24] Start people thinking of rightness and virtue in real-world contexts that preclude rule modeled on philosophic quest, and you invite frustrations that draw people to the ways in which government can impose social and political righteousness—in America's case, left-liberal political correctness. The question then would be whether liberal constitutionalism can legitimately foster socially liberal attitudes—whether, ultimately, liberal constitutionalists can demonstrate the superiority of their regime to nonliberals or even to themselves.

I have conceded elsewhere that liberal constitutionalists may in fact not be able to defend themselves to zealous antiliberals, at least not by rational means.[25] Sophisticated antiliberals know that they surrender to secular bourgeois liberalism merely by sitting at the table of liberal reasonableness. They know they cannot argue with liberals without

---

[23] See Murray, *What It Means to Be a Libertarian*, 81–89.

[24] See Robert Bork, *The Tempting of America: The Political Seduction of the Law* (New York: The Free Press, 1990), 254–57.

[25] Barber, *Constitution of Judicial Power*, 220–23.

accepting liberalism's rules about what counts as adequate evidence and successful argument.[26] These rules exclude evidence like God's holy word as grounded ultimately in foundational cosmogonic events that are essentially beyond direct or indirect human eyewitness, like the events reported by the unknown author of Genesis 1:1.[27] Sophisticated antiliberals know that liberals are not sure they can defend their rules because they cannot demonstrate, even to themselves, the nonexistence of authorities like the God of the Old Testament.[28] They also know that liberalism's view of evidence as essentially eyewitnessed and repeatedly eyewitnessable assumes theory-independent perceptions of reality that may well be (some say, paradoxically, "certainly are") impossible. For these reasons, so to speak (I have no other way to put it), antiliberals have no compelling reason to accept liberalism's rules about what counts as evidence and argument. And so they try to resist what they see as rules of liberalism's discourse. They hear what they take to be the correct version of God's will, but they try to close themselves to liberalism's secular reasoning. They cannot participate in what a liberal would term an "open-minded" dialogue without abandoning the essential elements of their antiliberalism: fear or love of God and unquestioning submission to his reported word, or dutiful obedience to the reported laws of other forces (especially "history") that are said to determine truth.[29]

This leaves liberals with two problems: how to persuade those who will not listen and how to persuade those who will listen. Racists and undomesticated believers have no reason to listen and every reason not to; bourgeois reasoning cannot reach them. If they are to be persuaded, it must be by some form of force, either the hard kind that Lincoln used or the soft, essentially economic kind that seems to have domesticated Catholicism in America, won the Cold War for the West, and dulled the sharper edges of racism in America. Liberals can believe that these developments constitute some evidence for the liberal theory of human nature implicit in Publius's famous statement that "the most common and durable source of factions, has been the various and unequal distribution of property," not "zeal for different opinions concerning religion . . . [and] Government" (10:58–59). The remaining question is how to persuade those who will listen to arguments conducted according to the prevailing principles of argu-

---

[26] See Michael McConnell, "The Role of Democratic Politics in Transforming Moral Conviction into Law," *Yale Law Journal* 98 (1989): 1504–6.

[27] See Leo Strauss, *Studies in Platonic Political Philosophy* (Chicago: University of Chicago Press, 1983), 148–49, 152, 156.

[28] Compare ibid., 151.

[29] See ibid., 149.

ment and evidence. These people, whatever else they might be, are liberal in an important respect: they accept liberalism's view of what counts as evidence for truth about the most important things—the things for which we tax, spend, punish, and wage war. Liberals must persuade themselves that hard and soft forms of force can be justifiable ways of persuading antiliberals.

Some liberal intellectuals have trouble doing this because they profess to believe that reasonable people can choose to reject reason itself and that reason has no escape from prerational assumptions that are culturally determined. But if we accept the second of these beliefs (no escape from culture), we must reject the first (the reasonable can reject reason), because then we are stuck with conventional conceptions of what counts as "choice," "action," and "reason." "Choice," for us, seems connected to a capacity for action and opportunities to act in ways that can go or could have gone differently. This capacity is a capacity to act for subjectively held or putative reasons, with "reasons" referring to commonly recognized goods and recognizable means thereto. Choice thus conceived, one cannot choose to live without reason, or at least one cannot know that one is choosing so to live. If someone appears to be living without reason, in some psychotic state, say, we can have no evidence that she chooses (in the present tense) to do so unless we have from her or can plausibly impute to her a reason in terms of some commonly recognized good. But if we have or can plausibly impute such a reason, she is not living without reason; there is "method in her madness," we might say. She can have a reason for doing something she will later regret, or even living a life of regret (as, penance, say). And she can, in a sense, "live" unreasonably or without reason. But she cannot *choose* to live without reason because choice seems to involve reason, and she cannot have a *reason* for living without reason.[30]

If we do believe we cannot escape culturally determined beliefs, then we cannot escape the perfectly conventional assumption of practicing scientists and ordinary men and women that we indeed can escape culturally determined beliefs. This assumption is manifest in the conventional belief that there is a difference between nature and convention, that nature is normative for convention, that true propositions correspond to facts beyond themselves, that no depth or breadth of conviction can actually put Pegasus aloft, and that no degree of political success can transform something like the Holocaust into a moral

[30] See Barber, *On What the Constitution Means*, 224 n. 43.

act.[31] The fact that these beliefs are conventional belies the suggestion that there is no accessible truth beyond convention, either social or scientific. Where truth-beyond-convention is itself convention, one can deny it only from a platform beyond convention.[32] Cultural liberals can legitimately tell themselves, therefore, that their views about reason, choice, and action may just be correct *and* demonstrable in principle even if not presently so. They are entitled to doubt that one can choose to continue living a life without reasoned choices about important matters. This gives them reason to believe that anyone capable of choice and free to choose would eventually choose a more-or-less liberal regime. They may be wrong, of course, but they have reason to believe with Publius that overcoming dependence on "accident and force" and establishing a government "by reflection and choice" fulfills an aspiration of the whole of mankind. And they have and perhaps can have no reason to conclude otherwise, even as they admit their fallibility and wonder about the limitations of reason.

Taking liberal constitutionalism as an institutional expression of a this-worldly rationalism and antiliberalism as rooted in antirational commitments like race, gender, and antirationalist religion), I have argued that even if people can lead antirational lives, there is no evidence that they can choose to do so. Add to this a further contention that a this-worldly rationalism is either natural to the human species or a deep-cultural commitment of modern Western peoples, and secular reasonableness becomes the unavoidable test, at least for "us," notwithstanding our concession that reason and her regime may well be wrong by truths beyond our (present?) grasp. This last concession is important; it argues for a large measure of toleration for illiberal private associations as simultaneously constitutive and corrosive of the left-liberal political correctness so feared by ideological conservatives and ridiculed, as one would expect, by politically correct left-liberals themselves.

Though I return to the problems of liberal tolerance and intolerance several times, I need not make every argument for liberal rationalism in this book. Here I need claim only what is evident in the Declaration of Independence and throughout *The Federalist*, starting with the first paragraph: American constitutionalism proceeds from rationalist be-

[31] See Barber, *Constitution of Judicial Power*, 223–32. The reference to Pegasus is from Michael Moore's response to Ronald Dworkin's contention that there is no reality that can assist us in criticizing the deepest of our beliefs. If Dworkin is right, says Moore, Dworkin will "allow Pegasus to fly whenever enough people talk about him enough in a systematic way." See Michael S. Moore, "Metaphysics, Epistemology, and Legal Theory," *Southern California Law Review* 60 (1987): 501; Dworkin, *Matter of Principle*, 162, 173–74.

[32] See Barber, *Constitution of Judicial Power*, 223–24; Moore, "Metaphysics, Epistemology, and Legal Theory," 497.

liefs, including belief in the possibility of large-scale social planning in accordance with the findings of secular science and through political arguments grounded in universal and therewith nonparochial human needs. As an exercise in first-order constitutional theory, my argument here proceeds within the tradition defined by these beliefs. Some positive constitutionalists who write in this tradition, like Walter Berns and Harvey Mansfield, will say that the best way to pursue ends like justice and the general welfare is to talk about them less and stick to a constitutional vocabulary of competing interests.[33] These writers are welfare constitutionalists nonetheless: they are concerned with the substantive ends of government, they offer theories of those ends, and they see their view of the Constitution as productive of those ends.[34] In allying themselves with negative constitutionalists, they say they fear the socially divisive potential of a constitutionalism self-consciously concerned with its purposes.[35] But no one has proved why positive constitutionalism must heighten social division. It is certainly not as if the negative constitution exerts a unifying pull on a population that would otherwise shatter into partisanship, for questions about negative rights and structures—questions preserved by negative constitutionalism—have always been connected to partisan conflict in America, and partisan conflict in America has always flowed from conflicting substantive visions of the nation.

Berns hardly needs instruction in this last point. In a classic analysis of the quarrel in *McCulloch v. Maryland*, he once showed how the debate over the rights of Maryland vis-à-vis the power of Congress (a structural question) grew out of differences between Hamilton and Jefferson about "the meaning of the Constitution," which he conflated with "the purpose of the Constitution." Berns described that purpose in substantive terms—specifically, in terms of Hamilton's vision for the country. "Hamilton's United States," said Berns, "enacts laws whose objects are 'to give encouragement to the enterprise of our own merchants, and to advance our navigation and manufacturers.' " "This is an aggressive country," Berns said, "busily and extensively engaged in

[33] See Walter Berns, "Judicial Review and the Rights and Laws of Nature," in Philip B. Kurland, Gerhard Casper, and Dennis J. Hutchinson, eds., *1982 Supreme Court Review* (Chicago: University of Chicago Press, 1983), 58–61; Harvey C. Mansfield Jr., "Hobbes and the Science of Indirect Government," *American Political Science Review* 65 (1971): 102, 107–8.

[34] I show this with regard to Mansfield in Sotirios A. Barber, "Reply to Professor Mansfield," *American Journal of Jurisprudence* 42 (1997): 191–92.

[35] I speculate about how an ends-oriented natural lawyer like Walter Berns can ally himself with a proceduralist moral skeptic like Robert Bork in *Constitution of Judicial Power*, 10–15.

many affairs, of growing authority in the world of business and the world of nations." And "[i]t requires an active government with sufficient powers to provide direction and to promote its interests."[36] This is a welfarist view of the Constitution.

[36] Berns, "The Meaning of the Tenth Amendment," 141–42. The internal quotes are from Hamilton's "Opinion as to the Constitutionality of the Bank of the United States," in *Works of Alexander Hamilton*, ed. Henry Cabot Lodge (New York: G. P. Putnam's Sons, 1904), 3:180.

Chapter Four

MORAL PHILOSOPHY AND THE

NEGATIVE-LIBERTIES MODEL

CONCEIVING the Constitution as a charter of benefits leaves us with important questions. What specifically is the general welfare to which constitutional powers are dedicated? When is someone well-off? What criteria determine successful answers to these questions? Are constitutional institutions and powers formally adequate to the people's welfare? Beyond these and other questions of constitutional theory are practical questions of how to apply theory in concrete legislative and judicial settings. These decisions turn on what are essentially scientific questions regarding the social, psychological, economic, and institutional consequences of different welfare strategies. What kind of help can normative constitutional theory offer judges and others who decide concrete cases? I turn to these matters in the concluding chapters of this book.

But discussion cannot move to the positive phases of welfare and the Constitution until the negative-liberties model is put aside. Though I have touched on issues of moral philosophy throughout, my chief concerns to this point have been the textual, historical, and consequentialist arguments for the negative model. This chapter focuses on the more abstract of the philosophic issues. The philosophic arguments *for* the negative model come as arguments *against* the benefits model. According to its critics, a benefits model offends the values of *fairness*, *democracy*, and *liberty*; it also confronts second-order objections regarding the existence and approximate knowability of notions like "welfare" and "well-being."

IS THE BENEFITS MODEL UNJUST OR UNFAIR?

We have seen that Currie and other exponents of the negative-liberties model assume that *if* government has a duty to provide police protection, *then* it may have a duty to combat hunger. Their opposition to the *then* clause of this hypothetical proposition moves them to deny the *if* clause, and that leads to an "unthinkable" result: no duty to police. I accept Currie's hypothetical proposition without affirming his "unthinkable result." I join exponents of positive government who argue, in effect, that the undeniable duty to police can argue for a duty to combat hunger. We have seen that Stephen Holmes makes the case in terms of relieving insecurity as the prime end of liberal government from Hobbes to Roosevelt. He finds that to relieve the insecurities of anarchy and civil war, liberal theory sought to justify unlimited monarchy. Relieving insecurity justified nineteenth-century liberalism among commercial interests that feared the regulatory state. And relieving insecurity justified welfare liberalism when dominant political forces saw the source of insecurity as the market. The value that justified the first step justified the latest: "[t]he *sources* of insecurity changed," says Holmes, "[b]ut the *value* of security itself remained the same."[1]

Holmes thus undermines the argument that only the negative-liberties model is just or fair—fair, that is, to those whose tax dollars pay for goods that, on a benefits model, others would consume. Holmes's argument both shifts the burden and changes the terms of debate. Those who cannot seriously deny a duty to police must now answer how it can be fair for the state to relieve some insecurities, or the insecurities of some persons, but not others. If the state has a duty to protect the weak from physical violence, why not, by extension, a duty to combat undeserved hunger? Those who answer this question in constitutional debate will eventually assume a benefits model of the Constitution. Because they cannot say that justice or fairness compels relieving the insecurity only of some persons, they must show how relieving only some forms of insecurity furthers publicly defensible ends. They might contend, for example, that redistributing no more than the resources of a state of nature (i.e., by stopping the strong from preying on the weak) promises more benefits to more people than providing against undeserved poverty in a market society. They might claim that while helping the physically weak in a state of nature eventually helps even the strong (who no longer need fear combinations of the weak), providing for the poor in civil society actually hurts them by destroying their initiative and independence. All such claims implicitly abandon the negative-liberties model. They assume a conception of the general welfare and a role for government in its pursuit.

This concession that government has a welfare function defeats any suggestion that the negative-liberties model is a dictate of justice or that there is a presumption in justice against redistributive acts. Justice disfavors redistribution only if there is some noncontingent link, either semantic or metaphysical, between justice and the status quo. Such a

---

[1] Holmes, *Passions and Constraint*, 257–58.

link is the only thing that could secure a presumption in justice for the status quo. No such conception of justice can succeed as part of a *constitutional* argument for at least three reasons. First, the Constitution displaced a previous constitution—a previous status quo—partly in justice's name. Second, the Constitution conceives justice as a preambulatory *end* of government—something government is established to achieve. Third, since virtually all acts of government are either redistributive or preservative of some prior redistributive act, if redistribution were presumptively unjust, no sense could be made of establishing and empowering government to pursue justice. Those who do empower government for the sake of justice therefore cannot agree that redistributive acts are presumptively unjust. American constitutionalists therefore cannot agree that redistributive acts are presumptively unjust; they cannot conceive justice in a way that compels the negative-liberties model.

Part of the current status quo is the market itself, in any recognizable form at least partly a creature of laws or law-laden understandings and practices that define property, punish theft and fraud, seek to maintain a stable currency, enforce contracts, and seek in many other ways to stop some people from using some of their resources (their physical and emotional toughness, their firearms, etc.) to get what they think they need and, by any admissible theory of justice, may even deserve. (An *in*admissible theory would confound the just with the lawful, contrary to what is implied by declaring justice an end of government and providing for constitutional amendments, which provision implies that any given state of the law can fall short of constitutional ends.) And because the market is at least partly a creature of government, Sunstein can safely observe that no sensible defender of the market can either oppose government per se or count regulatory activity a total failure.[2]

From this it follows that no defender of the market can sensibly oppose state-facilitated welfare per se, for the modern market itself is part of a state-facilitated welfare system, not an alternative to it. As with any such institution, it is answerable to the end that justifies it, and it is thus amenable to change in light of better theories of the general welfare and the means thereto. Nor can free marketeers repair to a skepticism that claims one theory of well-being is as good as another, for to do so would demote the conception of well-being that is linked to the market—that is, that one is well-off if one has the capacity and the opportunity for choice among the lawful pursuits of market liberalism.

[2] Sunstein, *Partial Constitution*, 5–6.

Is the Benefits Model Undemocratic?

The state's decision to benefit some segment of the population usually requires spending tax revenues for results that social and economic contingencies can make difficult to predict. Some writers have emphasized that the controversial and complex judgments of ends and means involved in these decisions belong to elected policy makers, not unelected judges. To exclude judges from such decisions, they deny the Constitution can be the source of positive benefits in the form of "welfare rights."[3] This is the argument for the negative-liberties model from *democracy*. This argument, note well, is not an argument against redistributive state benefits per se, for democracies can redistribute goods without ceasing thereby to be democracies. The argument is one against welfare rights *declared by unelected judges*. What makes the argument democratic, as some conceive democracy, is its background aversion to empowering allegedly undemocratic, because unelected, federal judges.

As long noted by many writers, assaults on the federal judiciary in democracy's name beg a basket of important moral and nonmoral questions, including questions about the nature of democracy, whether the judiciary can legitimately maintain democratic structure and principles against public opinion itself, whether the public appreciates the difference between preferences and principles, and the historical extent of popular support for the federal judiciary as an institution.[4] Also among these begged questions is whether democracies can legitimately constitutionalize aspirations whose meaning and worth are conceived as independent of social convention—whether, that is, a democracy can aspire to things like justice and the general welfare—for the argument against judicial power from democracy effectively denies that democrats can institutionalize a self-critical concern for things like (simple) justice. I trust that my previous writings on these questions excuse me from returning in this book to these long-debated questions about judicial power.[5] I observe in chapter 1 that American constitutionalists must assume that democratic constitutions can restrain pop-

---

[3] See, e.g., Robert H. Bork, "The Impossibility of Finding Welfare Rights in the Constitution," *1979 Washington University Law Quarterly* (1979): 699–701; Ralph K. Winter Jr., "Poverty, Economic Equality, and the Equal Protection Clause," *1972 Supreme Court Review* (1973): 100–102.

[4] See especially Dworkin, *A Matter of Principle*, 18–23, 57–65; Sager, "The Incorrigible Constitution"; Walter F. Murphy and Joseph Tunenhaus, "Patterns of Public Support for the Supreme Court," *Journal of Politics* 43 (1981): 24.

[5] See, generally, Barber, *Constitution of Judicial Power*, esp. chaps. 1, 4, 5.

ular majorities without ceasing thereby to be "democratic" in some legitimate sense. This assumption shelters *some* degree of power for unelected judges; as Walter Murphy has shown, constitutionalists must assume that democracy can legitimately support some degree of judicial power.[6] These at any rate are prominent among my assumptions here, and readers who do not share these assumptions might consider indulging them, lest every normative analysis of the Constitution be a work on judicial review.

Revisiting the debate on judicial power is unnecessary for present purposes also because no *constitutional* argument from democracy can speak for the negative-liberties model unless it is further assumed that the Constitution imposes only those duties that courts can enforce. The argument from democracy for negative liberties thus confounds *what* the Constitution promises and *how* those promises are enforced. The assumption that judicial enforceability is essential to constitutional obligations is understandable for a people who, perhaps of necessity, have become increasingly more acquiescent in the constitutional judgments of courts. But the falsity of this assumption is evident from the fact that though the constitutional text clearly envisions a functioning federal judiciary, no federal judge could even have thought of redeeming that promise before the first such judge was appointed by the elected branches (see Art. II, sec. 2; Art. III, sec. 1). Among the other undeniable constitutional duties left to agents other than courts are Congress's duties to appropriate for the decennial census (Art. I, sec. 2), Congress's duty to assemble once a year (Art. I, sec. 4), and the president's duties to appoint federal officers and faithfully to execute the laws (Art. II, secs. 2, 3).[7] These duties are incomprehensible if judicial enforceability is seen as essential to constitutional duties.

Later I deny that a benefits model guarantees that judges will do more for the poor than they will under the negative model. They may in fact have reason to do less. But I need not deny that judges *could* do more under a benefits model if they wanted to. Conceive the Constitution as envisioning the well-being of the American population, and conceive well-being as including goods like literacy and protection from the predictable violence of third parties, and the Supreme Court might well have held differently in *DeShaney* and other cases. In *San Antonio v. Rodriguez* (1973), for example, the Court may have found

[6] Walter F. Murphy, "Constitutions, Constitutionalism, and Democracy," in Douglas Greenberg, Stanley N. Katz, Melanie Beth Oliviero, and Stephen C. Wheatley, eds., *Constitutionalism and Democracy: Transitions in the Contemporary World* (New York: Oxford University Press, 1993), 14–16.

[7] See Black, "The Constitutional Justice of Livelihood," 1112–13.

that Texas did have a constitutional duty to ensure parity of funding in all its school districts because the Fourteenth Amendment imposes duties on the state (1) to protect all persons and (2) to protect them equally, and that these duties combine (in this day and age) to mandate public education for the state's children in ways that avoid discrimination against the poor.[8] The Court might then have adjusted its remedial powers accordingly, construing the "judicial Power," the "case and controversy" doctrine of Article III, and the Eleventh Amendment as needed to facilitate constitutional purposes. Robert Bork puts the point well: "If a constitutional right is at stake [amid doubts about the power of courts to remedy] why should the Court not issue a declaratory judgment, at least to exert a hortatory effect upon the legislature? A constitutional lawyer with the boldness to suggest a constitutional right to welfare ought not to shy at remedial difficulties."[9]

Bork thinks that his observation about judicial remedies tells against a benefits model of the Constitution. But why he should think so is not clear. If the best account of the Constitution should find a constitutional promise of benefits ultimately redeemable only by the taxpayers and their elected representatives, then why indeed should courts not "at least . . . exert a hortatory effect upon the legislature"? Bork's observation about remedies might tell against a benefits model for observers antecedently committed to a view of democracy that finds popular majorities doing whatever they want, without judicial interference, save only in terms of what some original majority declared in constitutional mandates. Yet even on such a view (Bork's own view),[10] what is consistent with democracy would depend on the intentions of the original, constitution-making majority. And there is no a priori way to foreclose the possibility that this original majority included a welfarist imperative among its constitutional mandates. In fact, I have been arguing here that reason along with text and history reasonably viewed leave no other conclusion. If this argument is wrong, it is wrong either because it distorts text or history or because it leads to no defensible good; it is not wrong because it offends values intrinsic to constitutional democracy.

This leaves only one possible argument from democracy against a benefits model, and I mention it to cover all the bases, not because Bork or anyone else has proposed it or would propose it. This remaining argument would have to exclude all Constitution-based judicial interference with immediate popular preferences. Such an argument would effectively reject the Constitution in democracy's name, for all sides

[8] See 411 U.S. 1; Marshall, J., dissenting.
[9] Bork, "Impossibility of Finding Welfare Rights," 699.
[10] See Barber, *Constitution of Judicial Power*, 3–5.

concede that the Constitution envisions *some* judicially enforceable restrictions on popular preferences. An argument that would reject the
very notion of constitutional democracy would belong to another debate. It would not be available to negative libertarians in the present
debate: they propose their model as a model *of the Constitution.* These
negative libertarians commit themselves to—even define themselves in
terms of—conceptions of democracy that accept constitutional constraints, albeit only negative constraints. They thus concede that democratic constitutions can remain true to form while restraining democratic
power. But if democratic constitutions can legitimately restrain democratic power, it is not evident why democratic constitutions cannot legitimately direct democratic power, direct it to good things like safe streets,
national defense, a literate population, and well-nourished children.

A successful response to this last observation can no longer turn on
a distinction between governmental action and inaction; it cannot be
said that directing power means governmental action while proscrib-
ing it means governmental inaction and that a difference of principle
lies therein. Recent writers have reminded us that government is always acting. When perceived as not acting to disrupt the existing distribution of goods, government is acting to protect that arrangement
through standing institutions that include the civil and criminal law.
Any given status quo results at least partly from government's disrup-
tion of some earlier status quo and therefore from some earlier redistributive act.[11] The assumption that government is obliged to justify
only its actions against the status quo and not its apparent failures to
act is a mistake that Sunstein has christened "status quo neutrality."
Sunstein finds status quo neutrality particularly offensive to the very
value presently in question, namely, democracy. Status quo neutrality
offends democracy, he points out, because it effectively removes from
continuing democratic scrutiny past political decisions responsible for
the current status quo and the law-laden practices that constitute and
protect the current distribution of goods (4–6).

Is the Benefits Model Antiliberal?

If neither justice nor democracy favors a negative-liberties model of
the Constitution, perhaps *liberal* democracy does. Michael Sandel describes the prevailing version of liberal democracy as concluding from
the fact that people disagree about how to live that government should

---

[11] See Sunstein, *Partial Constitution,* 3–7; Bandes, "The Negative Constitution," 2283–
85; Kenneth L. Karst and Harold W. Horowitz, "Reitman v. Mulkey: A Telophase of Substantive Equal Protection," *1967 Supreme Court Review* (1967): 55–56.

remain neutral among competing views of the good and stick to maintaining a "framework of rights that respects persons as free and independent selves, capable of choosing their own values and ends." Sandel calls this form of government the "procedural republic" because it "asserts the priority of fair procedures" for determining the public's posture toward "particular ends." He associates this form of government not only with center-left supporters of the welfare state but also with conservatives who view "taxing the rich to pay for welfare programs [as] a form of coerced charity that violates people's freedom to choose what to do with their own money."[12] In the name of such a freedom conservatives have opposed redistribution for a variety of purposes from old-age pensions under Social Security to national parks. They would have government concentrate on ends like law and order, national security, such instruments of the market as a uniform currency and the enforcement of contracts and, sparingly, public projects that "we would find . . . more difficult to accomplish" as separate individuals.[13]

Progressive liberals have of course long denied that big government in America has diminished individual liberty. Liberty, we recall, is itself something positive that can be secured only through power exercised against its impediments and for its conditions; hence Hamilton's belief that liberty and government are on the same side. Liberty was not denied, said Lyndon Johnson, by the Civil Rights Act of 1964, or by federal programs against poverty and pollution, or by school lunches, or by other programs that would liberate the individual "from the enslaving forces of his environment."[14] But further comment on this issue is not necessary here because negative libertarians typically see a role for government in ends like law and order and the legal infrastructure of the market. Charles Murray is an example. His case for "limited government" flows from a conception of "happiness" that finds "mindful human beings" enjoying the freedom to live personally satisfying lives and willingly bearing personal responsibility for their choices.[15] Elaborating this view, we recall, Murray approves state protections for life and property through a variety of means, including laws criminalizing assault and fraud and civil compensation for torts like defamation and breach of contract (7–9). Though fearful of the "ex-

[12] Michael J. Sandel, *Democracy's Discontent: America in Search of a Public Philosophy* (Cambridge: Harvard University Press, 1996), 4–5, 285.

[13] See Milton Friedman, *Capitalism and Freedom* (Chicago: University of Chicago Press, 1962), 2–3, 35–36.

[14] *Public Papers of the Presidents of the United States* (Washington, D.C.: Government Printing Office, 1963–64), 1:757.

[15] Murray, *What It Means to Be a Libertarian*, 18–22.

tremely slippery slope" that separates public goods from private goods (12), Murray can justify state provision of national defense, state regulation of "natural monopolies," and even state provision (through vouchers for private schools) of educational services (11–17).

Murray thus supposes that there are such things as individual and social well-being and that government can facilitate them. He differs with progressive liberals over what well-being might be, what threatens it, and how government can best facilitate it. His argument for "limited government" is more accurately described as an argument that government can do better, more often than not, through facilitating rather than regulating market choices and through avoiding those nonmarket transfers (taxes, conscriptions, subsidies, criminalized restrictions of selected natural liberties, and other forced redistributions) that do not contribute to maintaining the market itself. This position fits within a benefits model of the Constitution, and since that is the only model of the Constitution that makes sense, Murray should accept what it implies for the status of the market and the responsibility of government.

In a means-ends framework one's concern is with the *adequacy* of the means, not the least that one can do in attempting to achieve the end. Though an ends-oriented citizenry can withhold *unnecessary* resources from government to liberate resources for goods privately pursued, the criminal law combines with the civil law to obstruct private pursuits that are plainly incompatible with the ends of government. Neither negative libertarians nor other conservatives can easily reject this instrumentalist logic; they are not known for wanting government to do less than what it takes to realize their conceptions of individual and social well-being. When they believe government has a role, as in law and order and national defense, they show little principled reluctance to use the coercive tools of government to tax, spend, conscript, regulate, and foster the appropriate popular attitudes and beliefs, moral and nonmoral. Murray thus forgets about weak government when the subject turns to crime. Unlike today's permissive society, he says, "a libertarian society would take the few remaining laws extremely seriously," meeting criminal violence with "such certain and discouraging punishment that . . . almost all who try [it] will live to regret it" (7–8). Government should be weak, it seems, only when it comes to ends that government should not pursue.[16]

[16] For an argument that the American Right needs more than "little government" if it is to realize its own positive agenda, see James W. Ceaser, "What Kind of Government Do We Have to Fear?" in Arthur M. Melzer, Jerry Weinberger, and M. Richard Zinman, eds., *Politics at the Turn of the Century* (Lanham, Md.: Rowman and Littlefield, 2001), 76–78, 81–85, 98.

At this point conservatives might shift their ground and argue not against a benefits model of the Constitution in the abstract but against a model conceived in terms of *specific* benefits. They can concede with Murray that of course their thinking involves a benefit, that the benefit is maximizing liberty, and that the market state seeks to secure precisely this benefit. They can then claim that government's specifications of well-being beyond market freedoms diminish liberty and therewith well-being defined in terms of maximum feasible liberty. Maintaining and facilitating the market is good because liberty is good and because the market maximizes liberty by letting each person define well-being for herself. Governmental definitions of well-being beyond market maintenance either impose unwanted choices on some people or force others to subsidize lives of which they disapprove.

Judge Ralph Winter elaborates an element of this position when he says that the state's provision of in-kind benefits like food stamps and public housing for the poor "parades as an egalitarian undertaking" yet "has an elitist cast—noblesse oblige if you will—because it necessarily entails regulating the life style of the poor."[17] Winter reasons that if liberal elites felt the poor had good judgment and the right values, they would seek to provide the poor with cash rather than "adequate housing, nutrition, legal counsel, law and order, quality education, and so on" (70). He concedes that the poor seem to want these things because they consume them when available. But, he proceeds (in a way that could as easily condemn cash transfers as in-kind benefits), state provision of these benefits may be "indistinguishable from direct coercion" of "a life style" because the social resources diverted to governmentally declared "needs" leaves less for producing other things, thus making it more difficult for the poor to get what they may want most (72). Without mentioning what these other most-wanted things might be, or why cash transfers would be less diversionary, Winter concludes (with a bit of a hedge) that where "life styles differ" and government would cure "not absolute but relative deprivation," "no finite list of goods . . . can provide the cure." The state's list of goods thus imposes "the cultural beliefs of the officials mandating the distribution, not a shocking proposition to one whose legal training coexisted with the Warren Court, but surely one which casts the undertaking in a different moral light" (71).

Winter's position would be stronger if state-facilitated market liberalism were in fact neutral among competing conceptions of well-being. It is not, of course, and it cannot be. Market liberalism may, in a manner of speaking, "maximize liberty" at the retail level, but it excludes

---

[17] Winter, "Poverty, Economic Equality, and the Equal Protection Clause," 71.

life choices at the most comprehensive level.[18] Market liberalism offers more optional ways of producing and consuming goods and services than centrally directed economic and theocratic regimes. But a choice situation with more options is not always more choiceworthy than a choice situation with fewer options; it depends on many contingencies, such as the substance and scope of the options and their importance to the people involved. A choice between the hemlock, the noose, and the block (three options) is not always better than a choice between life and death (formally only two). But sometimes and for some people it may be. Though Socrates indicated at trial that he preferred life to death in Athens, he indicated later in prison that he preferred the hemlock in Athens to a life stripped of moral credibility in Thessaly. And committed believers of many stripes in many cultures, including America, restrain their own liberty to consume (and typically urge the same for others) in ways that their religions demand.

American conservatives should appreciate this last observation because the Religious Right and the white South are prominent parts of the current conservative coalition in America and because religious fundamentalists and racial purists should be the first to see something fraudulent in the doctrine that liberal democracy respects the right of each to pursue her own version of well-being. The exercise of that right, it is said, must respect the same right in others, and government should keep its processes open to all lawful interests and avoid giving legal expression to any one view of the good life. But such a system can hardly avoid discriminating against even some legally permissible conceptions of well-being (racial purity and religious zeal are not criminal), and American institutions do and constitutionally must deny the *full* representation of some views.[19]

The establishment clause, the Fourteenth Amendment, and supporting enactments and cultural forces thus preclude the full and forthright representation in Congress and the state legislatures of those who yearn for legally guaranteed Christian and all-white neighborhoods, not to mention Christian commonwealths and Aryan nations. Under the First Amendment, the Fourteenth Amendment, the commerce clause, and countless supporting precedents and expectations, statutes, and legally protected socioeconomic practices, racist and sectarian yearnings cannot be (forthrightly) expressed as laws in this country. We constitutionally cannot have legally exclusive racial or sectarian cities, towns, or even neighborhoods in America today. We constitutionally cannot use the criminal law to punish racially and religiously

---

[18] Stephen Macedo, *Liberal Virtues* (Oxford: Oxford University Press, 1990), 53–54.

[19] See ibid., 50–64, 258–59; Sandel, *Democracy's Discontent*, 4, 49–50, 66–67, 100–101.

mixed marriages. Because racist and sectarian yearnings cannot be expressed as laws, they cannot be fully represented. And the fact that everyone knows this explains why politicians who would represent racist and sectarian values are forced to represent them as something else. Instead of standing forthrightly as witnesses for their beliefs, these politicians speak in coded terms ("family values," "neighborhood schools," "small government") that implicitly diminish their beliefs. For persons who see in themselves no residual identity or "self" independent of legally ineligible racial and religious commitments, the Constitution guarantees no more than second-class citizenship.[20] These people cannot use the state for what they want most—to live in fully autonomous communities in which their values are honored in the most consequential decisions of life and death, ways and means.

In addition to a system of rights that effectively *disfavors* some lawful views of what a person and a life should be, the Constitution features structures of decision that actively *favor* other views of the good. The system of pluralist representation outlined in *Federalist* No. 10 envisions policy making by shifting legislative coalitions and therefore interests that admit of compromise. Walter Berns points out that this system redirects "the passions of men" from uncompromisable religious and ideological commitments to, bluntly, "making money"—"from dreams of heaven and glory to dreams of money." Such a people "would become tolerant, being content to live and let live, because they would cease to care about the things that men tend to be intolerant about."[21]

Amending Berns's account somewhat, I would say that people whose commitments run to or are compatible with wealth and the comfort and security of the body (as distinguished from the perfection and salvation of the soul) can see their views of the good and the right reflected in the gravest acts of the American state—acts like imposing taxes and waging war, imprisoning and executing criminals. America thus honors bourgeois views of the good and the right as implicitly worth the greatest risks, sacrifices, and demands. These views are not really hedged by a policy of live and let live; our bourgeois liberals do not have to tolerate violations of laws rationally designed to protect their values.[22] The commitments of some religionists and racists are different. They do not command the community's greatest risks and im-

[20] Compare E. A. Goerner, "Rawls's Apolitical Political Turn," *Review of Politics* 55 (1993): 715; Heidi M. Hurd, "The Levitation of Liberalism," *Yale Law Journal* 105 (1995): 819–22.

[21] Berns, "Judicial Review and the Rights and Laws of Nature," 65.

[22] I take this to be the upshot of Justice Scalia's opinion for the court in *Employment Division v. Smith*, 494 U.S. 872, 878–80 (1990). For a measured version of this point, see

positions. I intend my formulation as an elaboration of Berns's point. But described my way or his, bourgeois liberalism in America is not neutral toward ways of life in a way that precludes a benefits model of the Constitution.

The Moral Philosophy of Positive Constitutionalism

Philosophic objections to a benefits model of the Constitution can proceed also from metaphysical and epistemological doctrines. Well-being can be said not to exist as an objective property of personal or social situations. Or if well-being is assumed real, it can be said that reason cannot grasp or even approximate it.[23] Second-order objections of this sort differ from the first-order objections previously examined. To say a benefits model offends democracy is to take a position within a moral debate that assumes more-or-less objective content to notions like well-being and democracy. To deny either content or approximate knowability to such notions is to abandon the normative sphere in which they are taken seriously enough for their meaning to be debated. Metaphysical and epistemological skeptics may have much to say *about* the debate, but they have nothing to say *within* the debate.[24] They cannot even tell participants of the debate they are wasting their time, for that would ordinarily suggest that one should not waste one's time and that one should believe what is true rather than what is false, thus conceding things a skeptic cannot concede, like the objective value of one's time and believing the truth, and the truth of the proposition that one ought not waste valuable things—even if one finds comfort in illusions and enjoys wasting valuable things.

Reinforcing the dubious relevance in the welfare debate of epistemological and metaphysical skepticism is the growing strength among moral philosophers of a secular moral realism that affirms, through an argument that parallels the case for scientific realism, the probable existence or reality and approximate knowability of moral entities and properties like justice and well-being.[25] The most important potential contribution of modern philosophic realism to constitutional theory is

---

Christopher L. Eisgruber and Lawrence G. Sager, "Why the Religious Freedom Restoration Act Is Unconstitutional," *New York University Law Review* 69 (1994): 445–48.

[23] See Ronald J. Allen, "Constitutional Adjudication: The Demands of Knowledge and Epistemological Modesty," *Northwestern University Law Review* 88 (1983): 436–45.

[24] Ronald Dworkin, *Law's Empire* (Cambridge: Harvard University Press, 1986), 78–83.

[25] See generally David O. Brink, *Moral Realism and the Foundation of Ethics* (Cambridge: Cambridge University Press, 1989); Michael S. Moore, "Moral Reality," *1982 Wisconsin Law Review* (1982): 1061.

neutralizing academic denials of meaningfulness and rationality to legal-moral debates among ordinary citizens, practitioners, and jurists. These debates presuppose the existence of the entities, properties, and relationships (justice, well-being, etc.) whose nature and practical import are the subjects of debate. They presuppose, moreover, that these things exist (or can exist) independently of the subjective opinions or theories or conceptions of the parties in debate. This "theory-independence" of legal-moral entities explains salient features of legal-moral debates like the sense of the parties that they are doing more than merely urging their own arbitrary or subjective views, the assumption that it is possible for one side to be closer to the truth, and the sense that self-contradiction makes for defective argument.

Ordinary legal-moral discourse cannot proceed on contrary assumptions.[26] Yet a view popular in many quarters of market societies (which foster "toleration" by weakening religious, cultural, and aesthetic constraints on consumption) is that toleration is a virtue and that toleration demands a widespread "moral relativism." Without repeating here all that I have argued elsewhere, much less the far more extensive arguments of philosophers like Michael Moore and David Brink, let me just say that because democracy and toleration are themselves values, none but a moral realist can even hope rationally to defend them against other values or their better conceptions against inferior conceptions. A self-conscious moral subjectivist can offer no more than *his* truth or *his* feelings or *his* recommendations about the values in question. A moral conventionalist cannot hope to speak for more than the beliefs of his community; he will say, "Our views of democracy and toleration are good for us—or rather, *we think* our views of these things are good for us." And, of course, pure moral skeptics have nothing to say about things that they say do not exist except perhaps *that* they do not exist.

The theory-independent existence of at least some legal-moral properties and relationships, the separation of truth from belief, and the possibility of beliefs that approximate truth are among the defining tenets of contemporary moral realism. They also mark ineluctable presuppositions of everyday life. Their growing respectability among secular moral philosophers combines with their unavoidability in everyday life to shelter ordinary legal-moral debate from the varieties of moral skepticism.[27] Yet philosophic realism may not be skepticism's only alternative. Opposition to skepticism also comes from constructivism in ethics, which seeks to justify the assumption of objectiv-

---

[26] See Barber, *Constitution of Judicial Power*, 193–201.
[27] See Ibid., chap. 6.

ity in legal-moral debate by locating the meaning of normative ideas in conventional concepts thought to enjoy levels of agreement deeper than the debates conducted in their terms.[28]

Perhaps only metaphysical realism and a modest or relative epistemological confidence can fully account for normative debates like the welfare debate, for participants in these debates do presuppose that they are talking about things approximately knowable and real.[29] In any case, the truth of skeptical metaphysics and epistemology would be the only excuse for participants in normative debates to abandon debate. (I say "excuse," not "reason," for nothing normative can follow from the truth of no truth.) And skeptics have a hard time affirming the "truth" of no truth or approximately knowable truth. Skeptics are thus left with no argument for calling off the continuing quest for the moral and scientific truth about state-facilitated welfare.

Welfare and Moral Skepticism

A realist view of the general welfare cannot guarantee a benefits model of the Constitution, however. Ronald J. Allen rejects a benefits model even when assuming an approximately accessible truth about justice and the general welfare.[30] Allen rejects a benefits model because he opposes the judicial imposition on democratic majorities, which he calls "social engineering" and "moral dictatorship," and which he feels a benefits model would make inevitable (436–37, 439–40, 442). Allen says a charter of benefits is an "instrument of good" that makes sense only to a moral realist who construes constitutional terms like justice and the general welfare as referring to objective moral properties that are as "mind-independent" as "hardness or color" or other "real properties of nature" (436–37, 439). Though he denies that such a moral reality exists, he thinks he can assume its existence arguendo without weakening his stance against the charter of benefits. A "modest" epistemology (which he will not abandon arguendo) tells him that even if there were a moral reality, finding moral truth and applying it to concrete cases would be "too complicated for the Court or anyone else" (442). The fusion of law and morality demanded by a charter of benefits would leave us not with moral truth but with judicial impositions rationalized by "simplistic moral slogans that are unresponsive to the nuances of reality" (445).

[28] Dworkin, *Law's Empire*, 65–70, 82–83.

[29] Moore, "Metaphysics, Epistemology, and Legal Theory," 453; Barber, *Constitution of Judicial Power*, 187–92.

[30] Allen, "Constitutional Adjudication," 436.

I note in response that Allen's philosophic commitments lack the firmness needed for application to himself; he abandons epistemological modesty when advising his readers in a manner that reflects his own values. Wanting to avoid moralistic judicial impositions, Allen assumes that we can do so. This is a scientific-realist assumption; it implies that we can know enough about the world of human affairs to justify a course of action likely to yield a concrete institutional result: minimizing moralistic judicial impositions. Allen assumes further that he can offer his readers reasons for avoiding this unwanted result. This last is a moral-realist assumption, or so we can safely assume, because the reasons Allen offers are presumably offered as *true*. These reasons all have to do with what Allen assumes are true conceptions of real goods, like representative democracy, moral autonomy, truth itself, beliefs that conform to truth, and practices that embody such beliefs.

Allen thus advises his readers to "place responsibility" for defining social justice and welfare rights "in institutions that are subject to the will of the population," institutions whose judgments on highly complex matters are easily revisable in light of better evidence, not a "virtually unamendable monopoly" that would "dictate morality to us in the unamendable fashion of constitutional litigation" (439, 445). When law turns on knowledge, in Allen's view, the likelihood of error counsels deference to elected officials not because they are less likely than judges to err but because they can more readily change their minds. Where truth is the object, it seems, the probability of error favors the more flexible institution—presumably for reasons that reflect realist assumptions: because the more flexible institution is less likely to commit to error and more likely to move from error toward truth.

To decrease the likelihood that judges will review either legislative or individual choices in matters regarding welfare, Allen denies substantive benefits any constitutional connection that might serve as a handle for judicial action. He thus conceives the Constitution's enumerated powers not as John Marshall conceived them—means to constitutional ends like national security and prosperity[31]—but as no more than authorizations to act or not act, provide or not provide, as Congress wishes. For Allen, these constitutional grants of discretionary power do not imply affirmative duties to benefit. He says that constitutional grants of power do not "command[] the extensive social engineering" called for by the benefits model (437). As for the Constitution as a whole, says Allen, judges should view it as "a charter of principles of government and individual rights"; they should not view it as an "unconstrained instrument of good" (451). With this case against the

---

[31] See Barber, *On What the Constitution Means*, 78–82.

benefits model, Allen would reduce prospects for judicial impositions that reflect not moral truth but the subjective preferences of an electorally irresponsible elite.

Allen ultimately speaks (tries to speak) not as a moral realist but as a moral antirealist, apparently a moral subjectivist. When he grants objective moral truth, he does so only arguendo and as part of his attempt to deflate the case for the Constitution as a charter of benefits. Without argument and citing neither evidence nor authority, he ignores moral-realist gains in academic philosophy and the realist presuppositions of ordinary life and aligns two or three named moral realists against what he claims to be "virtually the rest of educated thought" (442, 451 n. 49). His personal view seems to be that "morality and moral judgments are constituted purely of individual beliefs that are not constrained by an objective reality" (439).

Yet, as we have seen, Allen's own argument contains prescriptive parts, and these prescriptive parts are addressed not only to moral realists but also to legal academe generally or "virtually the rest of educated thought." He argues categorically, not just arguendo, for a policy of judicial deference regarding welfare rights. He contends on his own account, not hypothetically as a moral realist, that it is wrong or offensive to democracy for judges to impose their values on the rest of us (439–40). As we have also seen, his contention cannot avoid trading on realist assumptions; it is elliptical for the proposition that judicial impositions are *objectively* wrong or offensive to a *true* conception of democracy. We have seen that Allen's own stance on judicial power shows no trace of his academic theories about morality; he suggests at no point that judicial imposition is wrong or undemocratic merely as a matter of his subjective preferences. Allen's stance on judicial power exhibits a property common to all normative stances everywhere, regardless of the speaker's professed metaethics: their assumptions are ultimately and ineluctably realist.

On assumptions more forthrightly realist and less modestly epistemological than Allen's, however, Allen is right on several connected points. Doubt, moral as well as nonmoral, does counsel revisability of judgments and at least presumptively favors institutions that can readily change their judgments in light of better evidence. And in a culture where the enforcement of constitutional duties is left mostly to judges, critics of judicial power may well have reason to fear a benefits model of the Constitution. Even on models of the Constitution that grant legislators and taxpayers *ultimate* responsibility for substantive governmental benefits, as the negative-liberties model does and as I join others (Michelman, Sager, Holmes, and Sunstein) in contending that a benefits model should, courts can still do much to help. Had the justices assumed a benefits model, they may well have decided *DeSha-ney* and *Rodriguez* differently, for example. Yet the dissents in these same cases show that the Court could have reached different results without changing constitutional paradigms. *Rodriguez* could have announced special judicial concern for the needy by declaring poverty a "suspect classification" under the equal protection clause, as Justice Thurgood Marshall urged, and *DeShaney* could have found that the relationship between Joshua and the child welfare agency amounted to a custodial relationship, as Justice Brennan urged.[32]

The question for our purposes, then, is why Allen might anticipate more judicial assertiveness under a benefits model than under a negative-liberties model. What causes him to assume that a newly recognized constitutional duty means more power for the federal judiciary? Surely the most likely answer is that he assumes that constitutional duties are enforced, by and large, by courts. If this is Allen's assumption, it is one that most Americans share. It is an assumption integral to their political culture, and it is firmly connected to the Constitution via the theory behind *Federalist* No. 10: that government best promotes the general welfare by fostering rationally compromisable pursuits like private wealth rather than trying to inculcate a self-sacrificing public-spiritedness. Elected politicians can be expected to abdicate their constitutional duties where their constituents are too preoccupied with private pursuits to develop a sustained constitutional consciousness and where the duties in question involve immediate benefits to "others" that only the public-spirited can appreciate as benefits to all.

While regrettable in some respects, moreover, this lack of constitutional consciousness may be a good thing on balance, even to the public-spirited. Publius, after all, claimed public-spiritedness for himself. A regime interested in domestic tranquility may well foster, as Berns argues, private pursuits that drain energy from the relatively more divisive and uncompromisable ideological commitments that constitutional debate often involves. Allen's assumption is thus firmly embedded in larger considerations, and rejecting it risks revolutionary disruptions that we should not invite as constitutional theorists unless we are prepared to welcome them as citizens and consumers. A first step in response to this problem focuses more tightly on the logic of the benefits model than on its likely consequences in cultural context.

The benefits model is intrinsically connected to the aim of any conceptual model: faithful correspondence to what it purports to be a model of. This good may be no more than a theoretical good. Its politi-

<hr>

[32] 411 U.S. 1, 117–24 (1972), Marshall, J., dissenting; 489 U.S. 189, 209–10 (1989), Brennan, J., dissenting.

cal value depends on a further assumption: that theoretically sounder constitutional judgments serve the general welfare better (in the long run?) than constitutional fictions that, in the case of the negative model, flatter the affluent by suggesting that what they have they got without government's help. This further assumption is hardly self-evident, of course; but I see no escaping it. I concede that it confronts a tradition that stretches from Plato's "noble lie" to and beyond Publius's statement in *Federalist* No. 49 that "the most rational government will not find it a superfluous advantage to have the prejudices of the community on its side." But prejudice presupposes truth, as does the distinction between noble and ignoble lies. And we cannot even consider whether, contrary to my further assumption, unsound constitutional judgments can sometimes contribute to the general welfare, unless we can hope to approximate a true moral theory of what the general welfare is and a true scientific theory of its empirical conditions. As it turns out, therefore, we have to assume a relatively sound judgment even to defend a practice of unsound judgments. And because such a practice, like all practices, would be defined and limited partly by what justifies it, unsound judgments would be acceptable only to the extent that they served judgments assumed approximately sound. So I see no escape from my further assumption connecting truer models, sounder judgments, and happier results.

Consider, then, how a better understanding of the Constitution's nature might have affected what the Court did and said in *DeShaney*. A benefits model of the Constitution would have made it very hard to deny that Wisconsin had a duty to protect Joshua from the predictable violence of his father. A constitution ordained to certain ends should be read to facilitate those ends, and the language and history of the Fourteenth Amendment easily support protection from predictable third-party violence as a constitutional end.[33] But a benefits model alone would not and perhaps should not guarantee *judicial* remedies in all or even most cases of state negligence ending in child abuse. Holmes and Sunstein point out that social services departments tackle enormous social problems armed only with "embarrassingly bounded resources." This resource gap virtually guarantees "that some potential victims of child abuse will become actual victims of child abuse, and the state will have done little or nothing about it."[34] They add that judges and courts typically lack the training, the staff, the budget, and other resources for "survey[ing] a broad spectrum of social needs," weighing "the distributive consequences" of alternative choices and

---

[33] Currie, *The Constitution in the Supreme Court*, 397.
[34] Holmes and Sunstein, *The Cost of Rights*, 94.

then "decid[ing] how much to allocate to each." Nor can courts "easily decide if the state made an error when concluding, before the fact," that one case deserved more attention than others: attending to Joshua at the expense of other children may have meant tragic consequences for those other children (95).

The Court, say Holmes and Sunstein, should have offered this "argument from scarcity" for its action in *DeShaney*. They add, as charitable interpreters of the Court's action, that a scarcity rationale rather than the Court's "shockingly brutal" formal opinion is "almost certainly" what moved the justices to dismiss Joshua's suit (94–97). So a benefits model would not have guaranteed a different *result* in *DeShaney*. But a benefits model would have guaranteed a different *opinion* in *DeShaney*. And because such an opinion would have left no doubt about a constitutional duty to protect Joshua, only about the judicial enforceability of that duty, the Court, with no offense to democracy, could have enforced a duty to implement the allocative decisions of elected politicians and taxpayers—a duty to spend the money presumably the way the legislature wanted it spent. The Court might then have permitted a jury to decide whether timely protection for Joshua was reasonably feasible under existing caseloads, or whether the Department of Social Services was simply negligent in Joshua's case. Holmes and Sunstein believe that Joshua should then have won his suit (96).

Although no rule of "reasonable feasibility within existing resources" could have eliminated the threat of judicial impositions ultimately on unwilling taxpayers, the mere presence of this threat decides no constitutional question, for the threat exists under many constitutional provisions. No one denies that judicially declared nondiscriminatory voting requirements or public schools may legitimately cost more than their unconstitutional counterparts. The same is true for judicially declared fair trials, humane prisons, lawful searches, lawful census methods, lawful takings of private property for public purposes, and so on. Aside from what the Court has decided on any of these issues, any such decision can in principle be constitutional *and* monetarily more costly than its opposite, at least in the short run. In a *constitutional* democracy, there can be no equation between impositions on taxpayers and impositions on democracy.

At this point Allen might have more to offer in democracy's name. I have tried to meet his argument from democracy by claiming that a benefits model does not depend on judges for enforcing affirmative constitutional duties, though contingencies may foist part of the task on judges. To illustrate and justify my response to Allen, I have related the Holmes-Sunstein "argument from scarcity" for the result in *DeSha-*

ney. But some negative libertarians might see something undemocratic about the Holmes-Sunstein rationale, and if that rationale falls to a further argument from democracy, my response to Allen is in trouble. The Holmes-Sunstein rationale may be undemocratic in two related ways. By suggesting that the taxpayers may bear at least some responsibility for what happened to Joshua, Holmes and Sunstein tell the good people of Wisconsin something they do not want to hear—something that, if taken to heart, would burden them not only fiscally but also morally and in a manner that implies the superior moral perspective of the burdening party. Not only that, if affirmative constitutional duties are primarily the responsibility not of judges but of taxpayers and their elected representatives (see 127), and if the Constitution is a charter of benefits, as Holmes and Sunstein might agree (see 93, 120–27, 184–85, 218, 221, 223, 226), then the American way of pursuing the general welfare more through competing private incentives than through public-spirited sacrifice may need some rethinking—another undemocratic suggestion to those who see noble self-sacrifice (one thinks of Josephine Shaw Lowell and Jane Addams) as more of an aristocratic than a democratic virtue.[35] The Court's rationale in *DeShaney* might thus be more democratic in two ways: it avoids the slightest hint of moral elitism, and it is consistent with the American Way.

This further argument cannot work, of course; you cannot argue from (the value of) democracy while insulting democracy, and the further argument insults democracy in several ways. The further argument effectively says that the people are flattered and need flattering by a false and senseless picture of their basic law, a false and senseless emblem of their political identity. It effectively denies the people constitutionalist competence, for no one can either reaffirm or understand themselves making a pointless constitution, and the negative-liberties constitution is a pointless constitution.[36] Nor does the further argument

---

[35] See Aristotle's *Politics*, 1278a, 1279a–b.

[36] One cannot reaffirm the Constitution's authority unless one believes that the Constitution makes sense and that rational acceptance of the Constitution's authority is possible. The benefits model makes sense of the Constitution, and the negative model makes the Constitution pointless, or so I have argued. I do not have to argue that one cannot reaffirm the authority of a constitution believed to be pointless; that proposition is safely tautological and therefore undeniable: Because pointlessness means justified by no reason (i.e., serving no purpose), you cannot have a reason for accepting the authority of something honestly believed to be pointless. You can have a reason for acting *as if* you accepted the authority of something you personally believed utterly pointless, but only if some agent (respected or feared) claimed to derive sensible prescriptions from that pointless thing and issued credible promises of sensible rewards or punishments for following or not following the agent's prescriptions. In that case, of course, you would actually accept the authority of the agent, not the pointless thing.

from democracy avoid the elitism it condemns in democracy's name. Those who propose that the masses need flattering falsehoods assume the truth of that proposition and thereby claim a virtue that sets them apart, namely, that they have the intellect and character to face a truth the masses cannot face. The further argument may be true, of course; Madison suggested something not unlike it in *Federalist* No. 49, and probably most (though not all)[37] present-day students of the Constitution would tremble (as I would) at the prospect of another constitutional convention. But true or false, the further argument from democracy is not an argument from democracy.

Allen might resume the argument from democracy by citing the personal motives of writers who propose a benefits model. Some of these writers may in fact hope to make things easier for progressive judges and harder for conservative judges. But if Allen could defend a theory of democracy that would make progressive judges less democratic, that would not make judicial assertiveness intrinsic to the benefits model. It is far from immediately evident why one cannot say that constitutional government in America is responsible for the common defense, the general welfare, and other substantive pursuits that the courts can constitutionally enforce either not at all or only in marginal ways. Nor is it clear why and in what sense we *must* believe that if racism, or extremes of wealth and poverty, or politically ambitious religiosity erodes conditions for constitutional government, litigation is the primary constitutional response.

MORAL PHILOSOPHY AND INTOLERANCE

If Allen should somehow prove that any and every constitutional duty to do good gives special license to judicial assertiveness, it will not be because assertiveness is either compelled or even encouraged by the moral metaphysics of the duty to do good. Allen correctly identifies that metaphysics as moral realism, and he initially seems to think that realism invites "moral dictatorship" by judges while moral relativism removes any "justification for . . . allowing the Court to impose [its morality] on the rest of us."[38] But Allen's more considered judgment on this matter is precisely the opposite of his initial suggestion, for he subsequently connects moral realism to a willingness to revise moral judgments out of a greater concern for moral truth (439). Realism's open-

---

[37] See Sanford V. Levinson, "A New Constitutional Convention: Does the Left Fear Popular Sovereignty?" *Dissent*, winter 1996, 51–56.

[38] Allen, "Constitutional Adjudication," 439, 442–43.

ness to revision of beliefs deserves elaboration due to a tendency in some circles of "educated thought" to link moral realism with moral dogmatism and moral antirealism with moral tolerance.[39] Because realism holds that reality is theory-independent—that is, that our beliefs are merely *about* reality, not *constitutive* of reality—it holds also that our theories can be wrong, wrong even at their ideal best, and therefore that we can hope for little more than (what appear to us as) successively better approximations of reality. This is realism, properly understood; and realism is not dogmatism.[40]

Realists are so far from dogmatism that thoroughgoing realists are— they constitutionally *must* be—somewhat doubtful about realism itself, for realism itself is no more than a set of beliefs about what exists and what makes for truth.[41] The very constitution of realism thus compels its openness to skepticism. Realism may in fact be a truer skepticism, a more thoroughgoing skepticism, because it is a skepticism about skepticism itself, an actively optimistic or hopeful strain of skepticism about skepticism. Realism is distinguishable from conventional skepticism partly by the latter's closure to its own fallibility—that is, by the nonrevisable or dogmatic and thus vitiated and paradoxical nature of conventional skepticism, which somehow *knows* that there is nothing to know, as opposed to knowing that it does not know. What the self-conscious realist sees as an unbridgeable gap between belief and reality gives her a reason *not* to assert herself, for assertion would imply a closure of the gap—a final and infallible knowing of something other than that she does not finally and infallibly know anything.

Because, by contrast with the realist, the conventionalist (often called the "relativist") professes to find truth constituted by convention, he professes to believe that there is no normative gap between truth and the community's deepest beliefs about "reality" (his quotation marks). The conventionalist therefore cannot say that the community's deepest principles are wrong, ever wrong, no matter what they might be or what they might become; and therefore he cannot say that dogmatic imposition is categorically wrong. The subjectivist is no better off. He cannot conclude that it is wrong to impose his beliefs, unless he just happens (arbitrarily, by his account) to believe that it is generally

---

[39] Many writers, even important ones, have made this mistake, including Jeremy Waldron, "The Irrelevance of Moral Objectivity," in Robert F. George, ed., *Natural Law Theory* (New York: Oxford University Press, 1992), 166; and Dworkin, *Taking Rights Seriously*, 160–63.

[40] Barber, *Constitution of Judicial Power*, 186–87; Brink, *Moral Realism and the Foundation of Ethics*, 90–95; Moore, "Moral Reality," 1104–5.

[41] Brink thus admits that realism may be wrong despite its present status as the position favored by the evidence; *Moral Realism and the Foundation of Ethics*, 127–28.

wrong to impose beliefs. And the drugstore cowboy who conventionally passes as a moral skeptic cannot (consistently) say that imposition
is wrong, for he professes to believe that rightness and wrongness do
not exist, anywhere. Realism thus seems to be the only metaphysical
position that can even hope to have reason to resist the dogmatic assertiveness with which Allen associates judicial power.

Despite realism's constitutional openness to skepticism and its insistence on the revisability of all judgments, two factors can explain its
appearance as dogmatic moralism. The first is a tendency among legal
academics to forget the distinction between morality and academic
theories *about* morality. I refer to the difference between the (first-order
or moral) proposition that, say, "cruelty is wrong" and the (second-
order or metaethical) proposition that "there is a truth about the
wrongness of cruelty." The moral proposition is indeed connected to
the metaethical proposition; all first-order legal-moral judgments presuppose a metaethically realist view of moral truth. All moralists therefore presuppose realist tenets regarding the existence and approximate
knowability of moral truth. And because moralists often tend toward
dogmatism, the stage is set for the inference that metaethical realists
tend toward dogmatism. But this inference is invalid. If moralists tend
toward dogmatism, and if moralists presuppose some realist tenets, it
hardly follows that realists as such are dogmatic. Metaethical realists
can in fact be systematically amoral or even immoral without compromising their realism. A realist can thus have what she feels is an adequate prudential ground for living a life she believes immoral, like a
life (Socrates in Athens?) consciously parasitic on a community whose
institutions she would subvert. What makes her a realist is not how
she lives but what she consciously holds about the nature of morality.

The value neutrality of contemporary academic liberalism also
helps to explain the perceived link between realism and illiberal dogmatism, for the claim that goods are equal suggests propositions that
realism denies: that, for example, 'good' and other moral terms refer
to the subjective preferences of individuals. Yet liberalism's vaunted
neutrality among goods is at most a neutrality among *reasonable*
goods, with reasonableness conceived as what is consistent with bourgeois values like physical security, material plenty, and equal opportunity.[42] Liberals tend not to count goods other than such domesticated
goods as reasonable and thus recognizable goods. Liberal constitu-

---

[42] Macedo emphasizes that major liberal philosophers are committed not to diversity
but to a *reasonable* diversity, and he holds it unreasonable for religionists to insist that
access to truth comes only to those who adopt their religious faith; see Macedo, *Diversity
and Distrust*, 170–72.

tionalism thus denies representation to religious or racial ends that would burden bourgeois aims like economic growth and equal economic and political opportunity. Disfavored religious ends include those that would invoke the salvation of the soul to criminalize the consumption of goods (forms of entertainment, styles of clothing, forms of education, kinds of food) deemed harmless on a bourgeois conception of harm. Disfavored racial ends include those that would deny (either by law or by legally protected "private" action) equal economic or political opportunity on grounds officially held to be economically or politically irrelevant or unfair.

Insensitive to goods beyond liberalism's pale, liberals confound neutrality among *domesticated* goods with neutrality among *all* goods. A cultural blindness to other possible goods invites the view that good is constituted by subjective preference, the subjective preference that liberalism does permit among "reasonable" or domesticated goods. The false nature of this neutrality has long been evident to those beyond the pale, like the radicals of today's cultural Right and the leftist radicals of the 1960s. Nor does moral subjectivism favor political liberalism over political illiberalism, for no general normative conclusion can follow from the premise that morality is a matter of subjective preference, and many persons have subjective aversions to liberalism, "political" as well as "cultural."

If any metaphysics favors liberal constitutionalism, it is realism. Because self-conscious realists must appreciate their own fallibility, and because they alone consciously suppose a truth beyond belief that can account for the fallibility of all belief,[43] they alone can consistently argue for philosophic pluralism. Philosophic realists who happen to be committed to the pursuit of moral and scientific truth have a reason to favor philosophic pluralism because philosophic pluralism seems essential to the mutual challenge of beliefs upon which progress toward truth depends. Realism's affinity for philosophic pluralism in turn favors some measure of political pluralism simply because, under modern conditions at least, a reasonable political pluralism seems more hospitable than any other regime to philosophic pluralism.

True, a "reasonable" political pluralism may amount to little more than a bourgeois regime that refuses full political representation to, and therewith full political expression of, antiliberal commitments like racial purity and forms of religious purity. Well might persons with these commitments feel oppressed by the norms of liberal reasonableness. I have acknowledged that believers can justly see offense to their

---

[43] Michael S. Moore, "The Interpretive Turn in Modern Theory: A Turn for the Worse?" *Stanford Law Review* 41 (1989): 871.

defining beliefs in the liberal requirement that political proposals be couched in secular terms. This requirement implies that God's (reported) will as such is never sufficient reason for public action, which amounts to closure to the possibility of revealed truth. This implicit closure both defines and troubles bourgeois liberalism, and therein lies liberalism's reflection of and dependence on philosophic realism.

Political liberalism depends on philosophic realism because, I have effectively contended here, political liberalism is but an aspect of a comprehensive cultural liberalism and, as such, presupposes the moral superiority of cultural liberalism over antiliberalism. Philosophic realism is the only metaphysics that can even hope to confirm (provisionally confirm) liberalism's implicit claims to moral superiority. Liberalism and all other comprehensive doctrines are the doctrines of historical cultures. The moral philosophy that can provisionally support the superiority of one comprehensive doctrine over others must therefore appeal to truths that are transcultural and transhistorical. This requirement precludes both moral subjectivism and moral conventionalism; it leaves only moral realism. The case for liberalism thus depends on the case for realism. If liberalism is or can even hope to be anything more than arbitrary convention, realism must be either true or provisionally more plausible than antirealism. And the greater plausibility of realism would be a reason to support liberal pluralism as a reflection of philosophic pluralism and as guarantor of sufficient intellectual diversity for progress in the natural and moral sciences.

Nothing in this argument for bourgeois liberalism will console full-blooded antiliberals who insist on actually living the lives they extol. They will see liberalism as a fraud not mitigated by its toleration of domesticated antiliberals, antiliberals who in effect profess one way of life and work to pay the taxes and fight the wars that support another. Guilty without question is that brand of liberalism that professes neutrality toward conceptions of the good life and thus takes itself excused from arguing for bourgeois liberalism. Perhaps little better, I concede, are those moral realists who try to defend bourgeois liberalism against forms of antirationalism grounded in religious authority, race, and sex. They challenge these antiliberals to a debate whose terms and rules of evidence favor liberalism.

The problem is how to avoid begging the question for either side in a debate that is of the utmost consequence for how people live. Liberals troubled by begging the question for their side cannot cure that problem by admitting testimony, like Genesis 1:1, that people can (say they) believe but that no human observer can confirm or ever have confirmed, even in principle. Realists who try to defend liberalism thus find their reliance on reason both incorrigible yet possibly wrong, a finding that opens them in a self-critical and continuing way to all but the violent forms of antiliberalism. Realists who try to defend liberalism may still be guilty of fraud, but their troubled awareness of that prospect may make them a little less culpable than either the dogmatic antiliberals or the value-neutral liberals who live their way at the expense of other ways while holding (for the galleries) that no one can rightfully live one's way at the expense of other ways. The case for liberalism, such as it may be (and not abstracting "political liberalism" from its cultural host), thus depends on the case for scientific and moral realism.[44]

[44] There seem to be two general ways to make the case for philosophic realism. These ways are broadly described as coherentist and foundationalist, with variations in each. A coherentist argument for moral realism in legal theory is Michael S. Moore, "Moral Reality Revisited," *Michigan Law Review* 90 (1992): 2424, 2511–33. I attempt a qualified foundationalist argument in Barber, *Constitution of Judicial Power*, 181–201.

Chapter Five

THE INSTRUMENTAL CONSTITUTION

WE HAVE seen that a positive constitution is superior to a negative constitution in several ways. Positive assumptions save the establishment of the Constitution as a rational act. Positive assumptions comport with the argument of *The Federalist* and therewith, arguably, "the framers." Positive assumptions reflect the instrumentalist language of the Preamble and the presence in the constitutional text of granted powers as well as specified rights. We have seen also that negative constitutionalism sacrifices sense without corresponding gains for such goods as justice, democracy, and decency. Negative constitutionalism makes sense only in a context that exposes it as positive constitutionalism in drag: the rightist welfarism that ignores the redistributive character of political action generally and holds the rhetoric of negative constitutionalism more conducive to the general welfare than the rhetoric of positive constitutionalism. My arguments to this point should suggest an uncontroversial conclusion saved from banality only by the currency of the negative-liberties model: *The Constitution charters a set of institutions for pursuing a set of benefits in a manner consistent with the principles of those institutions and a set of rights.* As between the benefits and negative-liberties models, the benefits model is the better model.

Our questions now center on "the general Welfare" that constitutional government is obligated to promote. What should count as "the general Welfare" in a charter dedicated also to ends like "Justice" and "the Blessings of Liberty" and committed also to structural norms and negative rights? These questions can be answered only by a substantive theory of the Constitution's ends and their connections to institutions and rights. Progress toward such a theory can begin by clarifying some of the formal properties of the Constitution as a means to positive benefits.

SOME FORMAL ELEMENTS OF THE INSTRUMENTAL CONSTITUTION

In two passages of *The Federalist*, Publius answers criticism that the constitutional convention that met in Philadelphia in the summer of 1787 both exceeded its charge and proposed ratification of the new constitution by an unlawful procedure. In February 1787 Congress charged the Convention with reporting back such revisions of the Articles of Confederation as would render the Articles "adequate to the exigencies of government, and the preservation of the Union." Instead of merely revising the Articles, the Convention proposed a new constitution, composed of three national institutions, an ad hoc electoral college, and augmented national powers. This new government was also founded on what the *Federalist* No. 15 acknowledges as a principle contrary to that of the old confederation: government that acts directly on individual citizens as distinguished from collectivities like the states of the union. And instead of merely proposing amendments to the Articles through the amending procedures of the Articles—procedures that would have permitted just one state to kill the plan—the Convention bypassed the state legislatures and dropped the rule of unanimity by providing for ad hoc state ratifying conventions and adoption of the new constitution by and among as little as nine of the thirteen states.

To the complaint that the Convention disregarded Congress's instructions merely to amend the Articles, Publius replies that Congress's instructions were "at variance with each other." He notes that Congress asked the Convention to propose (1) revisions of the Articles that would give the nation (2) "a firm national government" that would be "adequate to the exigencies of government and the preservation of the Union." He then invokes the authority of "plain reason" and "legal axioms" for a rule of construction that favors the second element of Congress's instructions over the first: when elements of a prescription conflict, "the means should be sacrificed to the end, rather than the end to the means" (40:259–60). His strongest statement of the end and its importance relative to the means comes five papers later when he excoriates the Convention's critics for asking not what power was necessary for the purposes of the new government but what degree of power was consistent with continued sovereignty in the states. This, he says, is a new form of the old doctrine that "people were made for kings, not kings for the people." The "real welfare of the great body of the people is the supreme object," and if the Union itself were "inconsistent with the public happiness" he would advise: "abolish the Union" (45:308–9).

In these passages Publius presupposes several related propositions that can serve as formal foundations of an instrumentalist view of the Constitution. Allowing for the controversial nature of judgments implied by these propositions, they can be formulated as follows:

1. The Constitution is a means to ends conceived to exist before its adoption and therefore to exist independently of its provisions.

2. The Constitution can either succeed or fail in achieving its ends.
3. Obligation to follow the Constitution depends on (a) the reasonably arguable progress (of the government or the civil society
   under the government) toward (b) versions of constitutional
   ends that all responsible segments of the population can accept
   as reasonable, if not simply true, and therefore as revisable.

Beyond its status as the presupposition of an influential historical
figure, proposition 3 results from any effort to make complete sense of
the declaration in Article VI that the Constitution (otherwise a set of
mere means) is the "supreme Law of the Land." We can agree that the
Constitution's self-declared legal supremacy need not make complete
sense to most people at any given time. Americans who accept rule
by constitutional authorities seem to do so, as Berns suggests, from
unreflective habit born largely of conditions that divert their attention
from systemic questions. These conditions probably do not ever obtain
for each and every segment of the population. They may not obtain
even for most politically active people most of the time, a prospect that
appears when one adds up the years of constitutionally conscious political debate stretching from the founding to Reconstruction and re-
suming in the years the nation debated national power over the economy, school desegregation, and civil rights. But the conditions Berns
describes do seem to obtain for most Americans today, notwithstanding emerging problems connected to growing class divisions and the
willingness of cultural conservatives like Robert Bork, Richard John
Neuhaus, and Robert George to question their obligation to a regime
that favors a secular political life and permits abortion, assisted sui-
cide, and open homosexuality.[1]

Yet the state of public attitudes toward the Constitution is beside the
present point. Proposition 3 is a normative proposition. It implies that
the Constitution deserves the allegiance of its people only under certain conditions. It does not compete with scientific or nonmoral propositions regarding how the public feels, the causes of obedeience, or the
conditions under which people generally are likely to accept constitutional authority. Publius can believe both that the most rational constitution needs "the prejudices of the community on its side" (49:340) and
that a constitution has no value other than as means to "the real welfare of the great body of the people" (45:309). Indeed, the content of

---

[1] By the present "regime" in America the writers in question seem to refer to the Constitution as interpreted by the courts and the acquiescence therein by both the public
and the elected branches of the national government and most of the states. See Mitchell
S. Muncey, ed., *The End of Democracy?* (Dallas: Spence, 1997), esp. 2–9, 15–17, 18–21, 42–
50, 60–61, 87–92.

the prejudice to which Publius refers is most plausibly that the Constitution is an effective instrument of its ends. This belief would lack normative significance without the further belief and the Constitution *ought* to be an instrument of its ends, just as it says it is. A strong version of this normative belief would be Publius's belief that the Constitution has no value other than as an instrument of its ends.

Because prejudice generally is unjustified belief that some proposition is true, prejudice presupposes that fully informed observers would confirm the proposition's truth. Prejudice on the Constitution's side thus assumes justifiable reasons continually to reaffirm the Constitution as means to the general welfare. Such reaffirmation is a condition for the fully conscious acceptability of the Constitution on its own terms because the Constitution explicitly claims to be an instrument of the general welfare. And since it is an instrument of the general welfare whose supremacy is asserted in Article VI, reaffirmation of the Constitution's instrumental soundness is a condition for the coherence of the Constitution's claim to supremacy, as Publius indicated by example when he rejected the binding authority of the (failed) Articles. Fully conscious and motivated fidelity to the Constitution thus implies a duty to formulate and work for the social, psychological, economic, and political conditions under which the Constitution approximates perfect sense—the conditions, that is, under which all responsible segments of the population have sufficient reason to affirm the Constitution as an instrument of their well-being.[2]

Realizing these conditions involves money and other community resources. And the duty to work for those conditions is a duty of officials elected by persons who pay taxes, serve in the wars, and forgo the use of their resources in ways answerable to the criminal law and the civil law. For these reasons more-or-less stable popular majorities would have to support the requisite conditions either directly as a matter of personal political preference or indirectly through attitudes or preoccupations that favor officials with the right values. At some level Madisonian checks and balances would not be enough to maintain the Constitution. From considerations of mere "personal ambitions" and unreflective private interests one cannot see, much less affirm, the Constitution as an instrument of the public purposes it purports to be. Constitutional supremacy thus presupposes some meaningful role for public-spirited leadership. And constitutional maintenance presupposes a measure of civic virtue (159–63, 169–85).

---

[2] My discussion of proposition 3 borrows from the theory of constitutional obligation developed in Barber, *On What the Constitution Means*, chap. 3.

This last proposition follows even on the assumption that the *general* welfare is constituted by the welfare of those individuals who make up the generality. Publius may operate from this assumption in *Federalist* No. 1, where he begins with an appeal to the "philanthropy" and "patriotism" of the reader and ends by inviting the reader to consult "your interest, . . . your liberty, your dignity, and your happiness." If the general welfare is an aggregate of individual welfares, the Constitution's promise to promote the general welfare is a promise to promote the welfare of each individual or each responsible individual or at least each generally recognized class of responsible individuals, like the "working poor."

This promise cannot be redeemed if the working poor are a disorganized and diffuse minority and if none but the working poor are concerned for their well-being. The need for virtue follows no less on the assumption (which I challenge later) that the general welfare is the sum happiness of the greater number, with happiness understood in terms of what gives personal pleasure, the more intense pleasure of some persons counting more than the less intense pleasure of others, however perverse or socially "irresponsible" such pleasure may be thought. If the Constitution promised the pleasure of the greater number, a citizen faithful to the Constitution would seek to promote *that end*, no matter what her other preferences. And should she personally prefer redeeming the Constitution's promise to all other ends that she might desire, that preference would identify her as a virtuous citizen of the Constitution.

Welfare as an End of Government

As an end of government "the general Welfare" is not to be confused with specific state provisions of the kind currently associated with the "welfare state." The latter are at best means to the former, though they can sometimes be means to other ends, like "domestic Tranquility" or even the control of exploited populations, as has been charged by some critics of welfare policies in the United States.[3] Specific state provisions enacted in good faith can also fail, of course, by bringing unwanted consequences, like dependency. The results of some welfare programs can also serve as evidence that improvements in the well-being of some segments of the population are practically unrealizable for any of several reasons, including the degraded material and psychological

---

[3] See Pivin and Cloward, *Regulating the Poor*, chap. 1.

condition of the recipients, insufficient community resources, or the community's diminished moral capacity.

A sense of fidelity to the Constitution as written will motivate officials to act in ways that help a population come as close to some model of human well-being as it is capable. All governmental provision assumes some normative model of individual and social well-being. Explicating and either defending, criticizing, or improving these models are all tasks of a mature and comprehensive constitutional theory. What these models should be in the abstract and what they should mean for concrete political decisions are connected but different questions. Though influenced by what experience discloses as feasible, the abstract model assumes relatively ideal conditions and actors. A nation's policies should try to approximate the abstract model as material resources, the character of the population, and competing values permit.

An important implication of these instrumentalist principles is that whatever the abstract conception of well-being, and notwithstanding the inevitable influence on its formulation of judgments regarding the potential of particular cultures, well-being itself is something to be described by general moral philosophy; it cannot be conceived in terms of the most that a particular set of political institutions is likely or even potentially able to achieve. If our best reflections revealed that the best life is, say, the Socratic life, that would be a hypothesis of moral philosophy whose truth-value would be unaffected by cultural limitations. Welfare as a constitutional end, however, will be conceived in terms of cultural potential. The Constitution being a self-declared law, the obligation to work for the general welfare is a legal obligation, and when it comes to legal obligations, *ought* implies *can*. The nation therefore has no duty to strive for more than its leaders are capable of grasping and motivating the public to pursue. And if the best life were the Socratic life, our version of well-being would reflect that fact to the extent permitted by our cultural conditions.[4]

---

[4] Such a prospect might not be as utopian or culturally eccentric as it appears, for Socrates lived and apparently wanted to live his life in an urban, commercial, and relatively democratic culture. He also lived according to a this-worldly understanding of reason (reasoning on the basis of commonly shareable experiences) and reason's authority over uniquely private experiences like dreams, visitations, and divinations—all of which are evident in his famous criticism of the Oracle regarding his own wisdom and in his insistence that the Athenian gods were constitutionally incapable of what reason disclosed to be immoral and/or irrational acts. For the rationalist nature of Socrates's piety, see Gregory Vlastos, *Socrates: Ironist and Moral Philosopher* (Ithaca, N.Y.: Cornell University Press, 1991), 162–78.

The essentials of Socrates' life may therefore enjoy sufficient overlap with central liberal commitments (to public reason and deliberative choice) to make the former a possible basis both for reforming aspects of the latter (higher education, for example) and for

But the *culture's* potential need not be the same as the *Constitution's* potential. The culture's potential may exceed the Constitution's potential, if not the Constitution's explicit promise. The general welfare promised by the Constitution must be seen as an end whose meaning does not depend on the constitutional scheme established to promote it. What the Constitution promises to promote cannot be synonymous with "welfare in a constitutional sense" because the Constitution, even at its constructive best, must be understood as potentially inadequate to its ends. The prehistory of the Constitution as well as its amending provisions and the First Amendment make sense on no other assumption. Why allow for amending or criticizing a perfect constitution?[5] The Constitution's reference to itself as "supreme Law" is no answer to this question; the Articles of Confederation refers to itself as "Articles of Confederation and Perpetual Union," and we have seen Publius prepared to "[a]bolish the Union" itself should it prove "inconsistent with the public happiness" (45:309). Keeping a lid on certain underclasses (in the cities, Appalachia, the reservations) may well be the most a taxpaying public is presently willing to support and therefore the most any American government can reasonably expect to achieve. But if so, the Constitution is failing in that respect, for many will deny that the general welfare can include conditions that millions of Americans consider either unfair, hopeless, or just short of intolerable. The constitutional regime (the government and the civil society under the government) cannot legitimately exclude these people, for they must be presumed members of the political community for whom the Constitution speaks. The Fourteenth Amendment makes all of them parts of "We the People," and they can legitimately be taxed, conscripted, and held accountable to the criminal and civil law. As members of specific classes they could not reasonably agree to these sacrifices solely for the well-being of persons in other classes. (Even if their agreement were secured through force, they would have to expect *some* benefit, like being spared more violence or a worse condition than their present one.)[6] The same holds for Rawlsian persons who have no prior knowledge of their circumstances and who are the moral equals of all other persons; they could not reasonably agree to a regime that benefited some classes with no improvement in the lot of the worst off.[7] Publius

---

vindicating the latter. For a discussion of these possibilities, see Thomas L. Pangle, *The Ennobling of Democracy: The Challenge of the Postmodern Age* (Baltimore: Johns Hopkins University Press, 1992), 119–30, 148–59, 183–94.

[5] I argue that a perfect constitution is a conceptual impossibility in Barber, *On What the Constitution Means*, 49–50.

[6] See Hobbes, *Leviathan*, II, xviii.

[7] John Rawls, *A Theory of Justice* (Cambridge: Harvard University Press, 1971), 14–15.

cannot be far from suggesting the same when he invites his anonymous reader—one whose relative situation Publius does not know—to consult his own interest in deciding whether to support ratification (1:6).

The abstract meanings of individual and community well-being thus prove to be questions for general moral philosophy, not linked to particular regimes.[8] Constitutional logic presupposes answers to such questions, together with the moral metaphysics they imply, regardless of what philosophic skeptics and conventionalists hold about either possibility. This should not be a controversial proposition. Publius opens *The Federalist* with an appeal to what he conceives as an aspiration of "mankind" and "societies of men" generally, namely, the human capacity for "establishing good government from reflection and choice," as opposed to a perpetual dependence "on accident and force." Moral skeptics, moral conventionalists, and some philosophic pragmatists can see Publius's assumptions as mistakes without denying their role in his thought and in the thinking of his readers, then and now.[9]

On the other hand, the practical task of constitutional theory is to approximate abstract truths in concrete cultural situations, which means to approximate them to the extent that actual conditions will admit. And the practical need to accommodate cultural limitations takes on normative significance in America and like democratic cultures where eventual popular approval is a necessary condition for a regime's legitimacy and where the Constitution makes mere means—mere fallible means—part of "supreme Law." This latter feature of the Constitution is a central but unavoidable anomaly whose mitigation depends on the extent to which constitutional procedures are thought to embody or reflect practical virtues that stand with the Constitution's substantive ends as independently justifiable goods.[10] Thus (recalling Publius in *Federalist* No. 45), it makes no sense to commit yourself to sets of policy-making and adjudicatory processes that may fail to secure justice and the people's happiness—*unless* capacities for practical deliberation and the discovery of truth are themselves seen *both* as ingredients of well-being (or as virtues by those who think it good to be virtuous)[11] *and* as embodied in the Constitution's policy-making and

[8] For an Aristotelian possibility with applications to the American Constitution, see Martha Nussbaum, "Aristotelian Social Democracy," in Bruce Douglas, Gerald Mara, and Henry Richardson, eds., *Liberalism and the Good* (New York: Routledge, 1990), 217–42.

[9] Barber, *Constitution of Judicial Power*, 192–97.

[10] Barber, *On What the Constitution Means*, 177–82.

[11] See Nussbaum, "Aristotelian Social Democracy," 221–22, 225.

adjudicatory processes.[12] This observation answers critics who claim that positive constitutionalism sacrifices to the general welfare "constitutional forms" whose observance is essential to liberty, fairness, and democracy.[13]

WELL-BEING IN AMERICA: A HYPOTHESIS

These considerations call for models of individual and community well-being that can fit a plausible description of constitutional arrangements and other cultural materials, and that seem justified independently in terms of transcultural values and expectations. Conceptions of well-being that seem both culturally admissible and philosophically sound can claim to be culturally appropriate approximations of some moral reality. They can claim to meet the conditions for legitimacy in what we saw in chapter 2 to be a constitutional regime whose overarching aspiration is to reconcile public opinion to the ends of government as real goods. I propose such a model here, and in doing so I rely partly on writers whose ideological diversity gives me some confidence in my proposal. But the soundness of any such proposal is beside the present point. I aim here to persuade the reader to my view of the Constitution's basic normative properties, not my views on how Americans should conceive the good society. My thesis is that the Constitution is an instrument of the general welfare and that as assumptions about the general welfare inevitably influence one's view of the Constitution, a sound view of constitutional powers, rights, and institutions presupposes a sound view of the general welfare. In submitting a view of the general welfare, I seek to stimulate a debate among constitutional theorists that might bring constitutional considerations to bear on issues of public policy beyond negative liberties and institutional prerogatives, issues like the income gap, the health care crisis, oversight of corporate governance, and the future of the public schools. I submit my views on the general welfare not to answer questions so much as to raise them.

This said, I remind the reader of the discussion in chapter 1 of the different basic strategies for demonstrating the duty of constitutional government actively to promote the general welfare. The "fundamen-

---

[12] See Sunstein, *Partial Constitution*, 20–24, 134–35; Nussbaum, "Aristotelian Social Democracy," 234–240; Barber, *Constitution of Judicial Power*, 216–18.

[13] For a spirited example of such criticism, see Harvey Mansfield, "The Formal Constitution: A Comment on Sotirios A. Barber," *American Journal of Jurisprudence* 42 (1997): 188–89.

tal strategy" argues from constitutional history, text, and logic that government in America has a direct and primary duty to promote the general welfare. This strategy treats constitutional provisions not as authoritative in themselves but as means to the ends of the Preamble (or, in some cases, as aspects of those ends). The "derivative strategy," by contrast, treats constitutional rights and institutions as preeminent. It shows how these rights and institutions presuppose certain conditions, and argues that government has a duty to secure these conditions as part of its primary duty to the Constitution's survival in good health. I have employed the first strategy chiefly because I believe an instrumental conception is the only view of the Constitution and its history that makes normative sense. But I said in chapter 1 that I would eventually turn to the derivative strategy; that point has arrived.

Our problem now is how to formulate a theory of the general welfare that can claim both cultural fit and philosophic soundness, tests required by a constitution that would reconcile the public to the pursuit of goods conceived as real goods. If we assumed agreement on a general account of constitutional institutions and rights, and if the only test of the people's welfare were cultural fit, the derivative strategy for defining the people's welfare would suffice. The substantive conditions presupposed by the regime of institutions and rights or essential to its maintenance could claim constitutional status. If, for example, an educated citizenry were considered essential for the operation of democratic institutions, which institutions government were constitutionally obligated to maintain, then government would be constitutionally obligated to promote an educated citizenry. Though cultural fit is not enough for a successful theory, the need for cultural fit justifies the derivative strategy for generating initial proposals that will then be tested against, and modified in the direction of, a philosophically sound understanding of the general welfare. Different assumptions about well-being would thus yield different views of how good citizens should be educated and what they should be educated to. Accordingly, I first propose a set of substantive conditions for the successful operation of constitutional institutions, and I then see whether these conditions can be connected to a transculturally attractive view of individual well-being.

Many constitutional scholars would accept David Epstein's assessment of *Federalist* No. 10 as perhaps "the most famous and highly regarded . . . of all American political writings."[14] As indicated in chapter 2, I follow Herbert Storing's view of *Federalist* No. 10 as outlining the

---

[14] David F. Epstein, *The Political Theory of the Federalist* (Chicago: University of Chicago Press, 1984), 59.

principles of only one of the two major parts of Publius's constitutional scheme, that dealing with "the tendency of the mass of the people to form unjust combinations against the few." The other part begins with Publius's criticism of the Articles of Confederation, moves to a call for "energy in government," and culminates in a theory of the presidency.[15] My emphasis on "energy" and power of course follows upon my contention that the ends of government are preeminent over negative liberties and institutions. Negative constitutionalists, by contrast, would depreciate the need for energy and focus on structural principles designed, in their view, not to enable government to do good so much as to prevent government from doing bad. Negative constitutionalists therefore have no reason to question *Federalist* No. 10 as a statement of fundamental constitutional principles. This enables me to take *Federalist* No. 10 as relatively safe common ground for deriving a set of substantive constitutional ends.

If I may remind the reader: *Federalist* No. 10 confronted the then conventional wisdom that democracy survives best in small, economically simple, and culturally homogeneous communities. Not so, said Publius: small republics cannot handle the problem of faction, especially majority faction; and the violence of faction has proved the mortal disease of popular governments throughout history. What is needed, Publius argued, is a large republic—a large population and a large territory with a multiplicity of interests each of which, to gain lawmaking majorities, will be forced to build coalitions with others. The discipline of coalition-building will moderate the demands of the several groups and thereby reduce the likelihood of majorities united on unjust principles. In an analysis that has now enjoyed wide influence among two generations of constitutional scholars, Martin Diamond showed that both the number and the kind of groups Publius needed cannot be achieved merely by moving from a small population in a small territory to a large population in a large territory.[16] A large territory with a large population does not guarantee a large number of political interest groups, much less the kind of groups willing to work with others in shifting political coalitions. A nation's interest-group structure reflects the psychology of its people, and in nations the size of China or India, people can easily define themselves politically in categories like poor against rich, black against the white, or Muslim against Hindu and Christian.

---

[15] See Storing, "The Problem of Big Government," 70, 79–85.

[16] Martin Diamond, Winston Mills Fisk, and Herbert Garfinkel, *The Democratic Republic* (Chicago: Rand McNally, 1966), 75–85.

Diamond showed that the system cannot work the way Publius describes it if people define themselves politically in terms of warring sects, classes, races, and ideologies. To see themselves as Publius supposes they will, Americans have to be a certain kind of people, members of a certain kind of society. In formulating this society's public policies, noneconomic commitments, especially religious commitments, will yield to economic considerations. The religious commitments of these people must therefore be either moderate or, when intense, privatized (79–80). This society will thus feature a multiplicity of groups, including religious groups, that will take for granted their collective power to criminalize fraud and other economic wrongs without assuming they can criminalize heresy and atheism. When thinking about politics and the coercive state, these people care most about property; among them, in Publius's famous words, "the most common and durable source of factions . . . [is] the various and unequal distribution of property." Diamond pointed out that because this society will need a large number of economic interest groups, it will need a complex economy and therefore an industrial economy, not an agrarian economy. To keep people preoccupied with their immediate economic interests, this society will be a commercial society committed to growth in both national and personal wealth together with economic and political opportunity linked not to religion or class—or race and sex, we can add, fitting subsequent developments into Publius's scheme—but solely to the individual's natural faculty for acquiring property (77–79).

Walter Berns, following Diamond, puts the matter succinctly and clearly: if the system is to divert people "from great causes to the small . . . from dreams of heaven [as per Christian republicanism] and glory [as per classical republicanism] to dreams of money," two things must happen. The system must produce "a larger and ever larger gross national product" that "can be shared more readily than the scarce wealth of the past," and there must be "a steady improvement in the material conditions of all."[17] And, in a statement that invites comparison with Rawls's difference principle, Diamond spelled out the implication of greatest interest here: "Indeed, it is especially the lowly, from whom so much is to be feared, who must feel least barred from opportunity and most sanguine about their chances. Further [Publius's] solution requires a country that achieves commercial success, a wealthy country. That is, the limited and immediate gains must be real; the fragmented interests must achieve real gains from time to time, else the scheme ceases to beguile or mollify."[18]

[17] Berns, "Judicial Review and the Rights and Laws of Nature," 65.
[18] Diamond, "The Federalist," 649–50.

I assume for present purposes that this regime of productive economic activity, equal opportunity, economic growth, upward mobility,
and religious moderation is a precondition of the Constitution's basic
institutional scheme. Moving now to connect Diamond's view to an
arguably transcultural, philosophically sound view of human well-
being, I must make additional assumptions: first, that the general welfare is in principle the welfare of each responsible person in the community, and second, that those who are well-off in this regime are
among those engaged in its "laudable pursuits," that is, socially functional pursuits. In the second of these assumptions I am not unmindful
that, as a matter of moral theory, and as a theoretical ideal, the truly
well-off (not to say the blessed) may prove to be those who are socially
irresponsible in the sense that they answer only to themselves or directly to some superhuman authority. What is more difficult to see is
how an irresponsible life can help define the welfare of the mutually
dependent mortals (members of the preambulatory "We") that the
Constitution promises to promote. Drawing on Aristotle's view of
human well-being, Martha Nussbaum says, "[W]e live to and with others, and regard a life not lived in affiliation with others to be a life not
worth living."[19] I say a bit more about this difficult problem later in
this chapter, but present purposes call for no more than a plausible
hypothesis, and in formulating such a hypothesis it is safe to say the
taxpaying public and therewith the democratic state can have no duty
to promote a socially dysfunctional condition.

As for the general welfare as the welfare of each, this assumption
will be opposed by social Darwinists and preference utilitarians. Now
a disreputable position that is rarely openly advanced, social Darwinism has been folded into a free-market ideology that assumes that the
present holders of property and social status owe their gains chiefly to
their own efforts without significant help from the redistributive state.
I tried to show the fraudulent nature of this claim in chapter 1. If that
argument is correct, we are left with a preference utilitarian objection
to my assumption that the welfare of all is the welfare of each. The
preference utilitarian would sanction the state's indifference to responsible members of some group or groups if such indifference would
serve the more intense desires of some other group or groups. On this
theory the government would be justified in helping the comfortable
and not the poor if the comfortable wanted that result more than the
poor wanted help and if the comfortable were sufficiently numerous
for their level of desire to outweigh that of the poor. As I noted when
commenting on the utilitarianism of Judge Winter in chapter 4, this

[19] Nussbaum, "Aristotelian Social Democracy," 222.

view of the general welfare, though arguably correct as a philosophic matter, is at odds with conventional morality, and that fact counts for something in America or in any regime where public approval is a necessary condition of legitimate policy.

A stronger argument against Winter is his assumption that a person typically desires what she thinks she desires at the time she says or thinks she desires it. No compelling evidence supports this assumption. True, if I want X, I want it because I think it is good or because possessing it is good, either instrumentally or good in itself. But when I say "it is good," I do not equate "good" with "what I think good"; I am not saying: "I want it not because it is good but only because I think it is good." And if I should say I want it just because I *myself* think it is good, I do no more than assert myself, typically for the sake of claiming independence from others who would decide for me, which independence I would assume to be a good thing. It thus appears that every conscious statement of desire has embedded in it a judgment to the effect that something is good. And from her perspective on the inside of her judgment, the ordinary actor believes the good in question is a real good, not an illusory one or a merely subjective one; she presupposes, therefore, that her judgment ("X is good") can be false.[20] If later it should prove false, she can sensibly say: "I thought I wanted X, but I was wrong."[21]

This fallibility of perceived wants tells against preference utilitarianism because what people think they want is often determined by a social environment that is maintained by established institutions of power. Nussbaum observes that the wealthy often feel dissatisfied when deprived of "the goods of opulence," and the poor have often learned to feel satisfied with their lot. She cites Aristotle and Rawls in behalf of this point.[22] Rawls counts as "perfectly obvious and . . . always recognized" the effects of economic arrangements on how people perceive themselves and their wants: "How men work together now to satisfy their present desires affects the desires they will have later on, the kind of person they will be."[23] If the general welfare were determined solely by people's stated desires, whatever their desires might happen to be, a tyranny could transform itself into a good government by programming its people to want what it wanted them to want. A theory that admits this possibility transforms the general welfare from

[20] For the realist assumptions of everyday discourse, see Brink, *Moral Realism and the Foundations of Ethics*, 193, 195.

[21] For evidence that Publius assumes this pattern of beliefs in his readers, see 63:424–25; 71:482–83.

[22] Nussbaum, "Aristotelian Social Democracy," 213.

[23] Rawls, *Theory of Justice*, 259.

an end of government, as the Constitution presents it, to an artifact of government. To avoid this result, I assume that the general welfare has objective content about which people can err, that it embraces the well-being of every responsible person, and that its intrinsic desirability supplies a reason to believe that people will desire it under optimal conditions. This leaves us to ask what constitutes the well-being of the responsible person, whether the social conditions of *Federalist* No. 10 are conducive to the general welfare, what beyond maintaining these conditions government should do, and whether constitutional government in America is adequate to the task.

WHAT CONSTITUTES WELL-BEING?

My chief aim in this book is a theory about the relationship between the Constitution and one of its self-declared ends: the general welfare. My analysis of the relationship in question has emphasized certain formal qualities of the Constitution, principally its instrumental quality. My theory is thus a theory about the Constitution, and as such it is indifferent to what faring well might prove to be as a matter of general ethical theory. I do sketch a theory of the general welfare in this section, but I do so only to start a discussion chiefly among political scientists and others in constitutional studies who have neglected the question in an era of negative constitutionalism. I hope this limited aim excuses the brief and summary treatment of what may be the oldest and most difficult question of political and moral philosophy: what constitutes well-being.

My starting point is the large commercial and democratic republic that Diamond finds presupposed by *The Federalist*. This society of *The Federalist* (calling it the "Federalist society" would risk a bad joke) is conventionally understood to be a further development of Enlightenment rationalism, which sought to found civil society on a theory of human needs that was truer to human nature than the theories of the pagan and Christian philosophers. When *Federalist* No. 10 finds diverse property holdings to be a more common and durable source of faction than religion and political ideology, it elaborates the emphasis that Hobbes and Locke place on mundane needs and goods like survival, security, and physical comfort—these goods over such higher goods as distinction, courage, and knowledge for its own sake (as opposed to knowledge for relieving the human estate). Testimony for this view of human needs is found in the horrors of the religious wars of sixteenth- and seventeenth-century Europe, horrors that undermined the political claims of the soul's higher needs (distinction and truth, especially about God) and put science and philosophy to the service of the soul's lower needs (peace, security, health, comfort). In its historico-philosophic context, therefore, *Federalist* No. 10 suggests that faring well is having desired levels of security, health, and comfort or having the opportunity and the ability to pursue them with reasonable success if one wants to.

Faring well in this commercially productive democracy of equal opportunity and general upward mobility requires the moral, intellectual, and material capacities for intelligent participation in the community's affairs and choice among vocations that promise personal wealth sufficient for things like decent housing, adequate nutrition, health care, the education of one's children, some saving, some play, and a secure old age. Faring well in this society might best be viewed not as actually possessing good things (Joshua DeShaney may now be decently housed and well fed) but as developing or possessing the capacity to get them by one's lawful efforts to the extent that one reasonably wants. Publius thus says (10:58) that the first object of government is not protecting property but protecting the different and unequal *faculties* for acquiring property. This resonates with Nussbaum's argument that faring well consists more in the ability to get good things than in possessing them.[24] Faring well in this society is compatible with religious commitments that bourgeois liberalism finds reasonable (more on this momentarily). But given the First and Fourteenth Amendments, faring well here cannot require use of the criminal law to secure environments favoring sectarian observance or racist or sexist domination. Nor are persons with an overpowering concern for their neighbors' sexual morality likely to fare well here, for by encouraging the demand for new goods and services, a "growth" society relaxes aesthetic and religious restraints on the appetites generally and on how individuals imagine and express themselves.[25] And this society's economic commitments may yet prove incompatible with what Nussbaum calls several other "very basic" human needs, like the opportunity to live with concern for other species and the undeveloped natural world and the capacity to form strong friendships, family relations, and civic relations.[26]

Behind all theories of what constitutes well-being and who fares well we find assumptions about who fares best. Those who think faring

---

[24] Nussbaum, "Aristotelian Social Democracy," 208–14.

[25] Compare Macedo, *Diversity and Distrust*, 181.

[26] Nussbaum, "Aristotelian Social Democracy," 222–23, 225. For a disturbing account of how advanced market democracies are eroding friendships, family solidarity, and trust in political institutions, see Robert E. Lane, *The Loss of Happiness in Market Democracies* (New Haven, Conn.: Yale University Press, 2000), esp. chaps. 5–6.

well is getting what one wants, whatever one might want, assume that the life of an omnipotent being is the best life. They assume this because only omnipotence could close the gap between what one thinks one wants and what one really wants or what is truly worth wanting. For one with power fully to determine the nature and goodness of a thing and the nature of goodness itself, there is no gap between opinion and truth about the good. And only the omnipotent could get and keep whatever she wants. Then there is the life of one who knows that he has little more than mere opinions about what is good and yet cannot help assuming a difference between real and apparent goods. This person, though aware of his fallibility, may also believe that he is educable. Plato's Socrates is such a character. Let me say a few things about these two lives.

By his own account Plato's Socrates is parasitic on society, and in many ways. A reflective creature of mortal flesh in a world of limited resources, he depends on organized society to live a life he can recognize as human. Beyond his bodily, procreative, and recreational needs, he needs the opinions of others regarding matters about which he seeks the truth that lies beyond his own opinions. His need for these other opinions is a need for friendly conversations. Friendly conversations cannot occur where the rejection of an opinion condemns its defender to loss of life, liberty, or property. Because philosophic inquiry into the most serious questions typically occurs in social settings whose supporting norms of civil accountability assume and depend on answers to the very questions in philosophic play, philosophy thrives in institutional form only where it is seen by nonphilosophers as a kind of play. The society that permits (and thus supports) philosophy must be secure enough in its own principles to see questioning them as relatively harmless. When working as planned, the society of the *Federalist* No. 10 is such a society. Its material pursuits and rewards are sufficiently engrossing to make the state relatively indifferent to debates among academic philosophers and theologians. And the academics themselves must have reasons either to approve bourgeois liberalism or to refrain from opposing it in ways that present a political threat. These reasons would involve the attractions and nearly pervasive power of bourgeois liberalism, doubt that God rewards antiliberal martyrs, and the opportunity for philosophers to live and play here.

Socratics can support bourgeois liberalism for still another reason; by "reason" both refer to *experiential* reason—reason that appeals ultimately not to hearsay or the privileged experiences of this or that tradition or tribe about the genesis of the cosmos, but to phenomena that, in principle, are repeatedly observable by all competent human beings.[27] The state that maintains bourgeois liberalism would help its citizens fare well by giving those of it citizens who want it the opportunity to fare best, the opportunity, that is, to live a philosophic life that is different from the bourgeois life. Diamond believed that the framers took for granted that the "full range of higher human virtues would have suitable opportunity to flourish ... privately" in bourgeois America. He said that "one should also note gratefully that the American political order, with its heterogeneous and fluctuating majorities and with its principle of liberty, supplies a not inhospitable home to the love of learning"—notwithstanding the "respectable distance" between this love of learning and the Constitution's "policy of opposite and rival interests."[28]

Yet, opportunity or no, few if any will live philosophic lives, for few if any can. The Socratic character will want eventually to question not just a society's prevailing political, economic, and social arrangements, but all of its controlling beliefs, including the very beliefs that enable him to ask meaningful questions. Because questioning all such beliefs seems conceptually and psychologically impossible, the philosopher's ambition seems fruitless and thus frustrating, sometimes even dangerously so. For these reasons, it is easier to believe that he who fares best is, in principle, the omnipotent being mentioned earlier. And though the existence of such a being is at least as problematic as the existence of the Platonic Socrates, plausibility becomes less a problem when we project the relevant qualities of the omnipotent being onto the human plane. The best human life now appears to us as the life of one who, by her own choice and capacity, gets what she (thinks she) wants, or what she reasonably (thinks she) wants.

On this last assumption, a government that would promote the general welfare would be a government that would do what it reasonably could to maximize the capacities of its people to pursue reasonable wants. The feasibility of any such policy depends in part on the *reasonableness* of wants. The differences between these people would have to be relatively superficial for them to live and pull together in peace and war. Bourgeois liberalism is such a society if we take reasonableness to be *experiential* or *this-worldly reasonableness*. So the society of *Federalist* No. 10 may promote the general welfare on two fundamentally different views of who fares best, a socialized, godlike human being and

[27] For this interpretation of the difference between what the God-fearing take as evidence and what the philosopher-scientist takes as evidence, see Leo Strauss, "An Interpretation of Genesis," *L'Homme* 21 (1981): 6–8, 18–20.

[28] Martin Diamond, "Ethics and Politics: The American Way," in Robert H. Horwitz, ed., *The Moral Foundations of the American Republic* (Charlottesville: University Press of Virginia, 1986), 103–4, 107–8.

the Socratic character. The society of *Federalist* No. 10 cannot actively promote the life of politicized (as opposed to domesticated or privatized) religiosity, racism, or sexism.

Liberalism's limited hospitality to moral disagreement and moral inquiry has implications for the question whether liberalism can defend itself against antiliberalism. Bourgeois liberals themselves may not be able to justify opposition to nondomesticated forms of antiliberalism. Liberalism is a way of living that, with other ways of living, proceeds from assumptions about what is good. These assumptions cannot be examined at the same time that they are being acted upon. Examining beliefs seriously necessitates being open to their rejection, and to the extent that one is prepared to reject liberalism, one is not simply and unequivocally a liberal. Liberals as such cannot fully defend liberalism. And those who cannot defend liberalism cannot really know whether the bourgeois life is a good life. If I may modify a borrowed thought, those who cannot examine the assumptions of their lives cannot know whether their lives are worth living. Philosophers who bring Socrates' method and attitude to social concerns are therefore the only persons who can even hope to know whether a life is worth living; these philosophers are the only ones who can even hope to defend bourgeois liberalism or any other regime. This still does not answer our question, however: Can anyone defend liberalism's opposition to antiliberalism?

Though *favoring* a regime is certainly different from *defending* a regime, it helps to recall the reasons Socratics can favor liberalism: liberalism's provision of the conditions for philosophic and scientific inquiry and its assumption that reason is experiential reason. Socratics can favor bourgeois modernity as long as it provides a place that is congenial to their pursuits, and bourgeois liberalism does this by permitting (and therewith supporting) such institutions and practices as secular science; relatively free academic inquiry and artistic expression; some religious pluralism; and equal economic, social, and political opportunities regardless of race, sex, sexual preference, cultural origin, or other differences unrelated to the intellectual capacity to function in "laudable pursuits." The Socratic can thus see bourgeois modernity as something of a fusion of Socratic reason and a godlike view of the good life. This is the good life initially seen as getting what one wants or enjoying the power to get what one wants and subsequently (i.e., on reflection about the social character and limitations of human power) enjoying both the capacity and the opportunity to get what one *reasonably* wants. The reasonable here is reasonable in two related senses: that which meets tests of accountability to a whole and functioning community of other persons, and that which appeals to what all humans as such can see as the likely truth about themselves and the world—their common mortality, for example, and their common needs for things like nourishment, society, and something to call one's own.[29]

No one can justify this kind of reasonableness to persons who act as if the test of justified belief is not the experiences they share in principle with all other persons but what comes to them solely by some particular religious or ethnic tradition or by virtue of their race or sex. A world of antagonistic cultures marks the most immediate problem in defining the general welfare. This problem is compounded where the general welfare is assumed to be the well-being of each responsible member of the community, for individuals can differ among themselves over who fares well. Yet far from precluding progress, cultural and intracultural disagreements presuppose its possibility. For persons who debate the meaning of well-being presuppose both a truth of the matter and that one side can get closer to the truth. Conversational disagreements, as opposed to either violent or silent disagreements, also assume that a dialectical process is the best way to pursue the truth. By a dialectical disagreement I mean the process of inquiry that Rawls describes and the Platonic Socrates illustrates: good-faith disagreements that go back and forth, testing generalizations and particular beliefs against each other until both sides settle on a conception that they believe needs no further testing, for the time being and the purposes at hand. Dialectical disagreement presupposes common experiences, and common experiences imply a community of perception, assessment, and purpose or need (including need for the truth). Where disagreement is either wholly violent or silent, an observer has no evidence that the disagreement is reasonable, for neither side offers reasons. And if only one side is willing to offer reasons, it has no evidence that the other side is reasonable. The reasoning side has no evidence that those who will not listen can reasonably disagree.

Reasonable disagreement thus conceived anticipates a secular view of well-being. Dialectic rules out appeals to evidence deemed privileged to only one of two interlocutors; for this reason it precludes privileged evidence generally, evidence that, in principle, is evident only to some human beings or to none at all. Because dialectic disfavors evidence that is privileged or cannot possibly be more than hearsay, it disfavors reports regarding the world's presumed origins that cannot be confirmed by inference from what is accessible in principle to physically and mentally sound human beings at all times everywhere. Socratics can accept the cosmogony of the big bang; they cannot accept

---

[29] Nussbaum can thus derive support for liberalism's emphasis on choice from Aristotle's conception of faring well to meet universal human needs. See "Aristotelian Social Democracy," 213–14.

the cosmogony of Genesis because they cannot make sense of it.[30] This does not prove the story told in Genesis is untrue, for it may be true, albeit unlikely, and all save those who say "(it is true that) truth is human artifact" will admit that truth *may* be (almost surely is) beyond human grasp. What is precluded is the story of Genesis as foundational for how every reasonable person ought to live, for dialectic favors conclusions demonstrable in principle to all sides of good-faith efforts to approach truth. And even if true, Genesis is hardly an inference from the physical phenomena that, we must and do assume, are accessible to human beings as such, regardless of sectarian commitment. For the same reason, dialectic rules out normative appeals to experiences that are altogether and in principle confined to members of particular racial, ethnic, and sexual groups. Dialectic favors evidence from universally sharable experiences. Nussbaum lists these experiences as those relating to the human body (hunger, thirst, pleasure, pain); human mortality; forms of human sociability; the dependency of children; the basic cognitive functions of the human mind; the pleasures of play; the capacity to recognize other human beings; and the physical and psychological separateness of each individual, a separateness that manifests itself in the identity of individuals as unique personalities and in their desire to call something their own.[31]

So however well-being is conceived, a reasonable conception must refer to commonalties like the ones just enumerated. And though this suggestion may well show once again that "reasonableness" is little more than a vehicle for imposing bourgeois values, this insight does not show how we can do without reason and reasonableness or how privileged evidence can function as evidence. Nor does it make silence or violence or sectarian or racist appeals any less unreasonable. However packaged, the refusal of others to listen cannot constitute a reason for rejecting reason. Supporting this conclusion is the impossibility of actively or voluntarily rejecting reason—impossible, as we have seen, because of what counts as behaving actively and voluntarily. We do not see a person acting unless we impute to him a reason in terms of what he thinks good, which good is something we can agree is at least an apparent good. If our neighbor Abraham is blowing himself up, or handling venomous snakes, or plunging a knife into his young son Isaac while under no apparent duress, we will surely say, no matter what his stated reason, that he is acting under the compulsion of mental disorder, and therefore not acting so much as suffering.

[30] See Strauss, "An Interpretation of Genesis," 17–18, 20.
[31] See Nussbaum, "Aristotelian Social Democracy," 217–26.

We would have to admit, on the other hand, that what counts as voluntary action is what counts *with us*. We would also have to admit that disturbed though he seems, Abraham *could* be acting voluntarily and for the best of reasons, even if we cannot confirm those reasons against our own experiences. This last admission would trouble us because reasonable persons must appreciate their own fallibility, and this would move us to tolerate Abraham's beliefs to the extent that we reasonably could—that is, if there were little danger of his or anyone else's acting on them. Under some circumstances, therefore, we should permit him to say and even teach that sometimes it is right to kill a helpless child. We might even protect his opportunity to kill the child by not removing the child from his custody or restraining him simply for the abstract thought that precedes the murderous act. The First, the Fifth, and the Fourteenth Amendments combine to guarantee all these benefits—including Abraham's opportunity to choose between right and wrong. (Abraham's case would differ from Randy DeShaney's. Because the Department of Social Services had evidence that DeShaney had repeatedly beaten Joshua, the First Amendment would not have protected DeShaney from loss of custody.) But there are limits to reasonable tolerance, even if we have doubts about what is truly reasonable. Precisely because Abraham's reasons are privileged—not grounded in common experience or plausibly in goods commonly recognizable as more compelling than Isaac's life—they cannot function as reasons for us, and we cannot reasonably refuse to define Isaac's killing as a punishable murder. Nor can we reasonably refuse to stop Abraham in the actual commission of the deed if we have an opportunity to do so without risk to ourselves. We may be wrong in seeing his act as murder and in trying to stop him, but the evidence in our possession justifies the conclusion, however provisional, that we are probably not wrong. Abraham offers nothing we can appreciate as evidence to the contrary, and we simply cannot help accepting what survives our best self-critical effort as the better evidence.

In light of these reflections one can hypothesize that a person is well-off if she enjoys the material, emotional, and intellectual wherewithal to engage, if she wants to, in the laudable or at least harmless pursuits of a bourgeois-liberal community, *and* that such a person is better off than her counterparts in antiliberal communities whose common feature is hostility to secular reasonableness among reasonably autonomous persons—hostility, that is, to thinking for oneself and with others on the basis of commonly recognized goods and sharable experiences. Because government must maintain the conditions for developing and exercising the capacities in whose possession well-being consists, well-being in America would also include the education, economic independence, and self-respect sufficient for the electoral choices that the Constitution envisions. These civic ingredients of well-being are justified also in terms of goods rooted either in human nature or in conventions deep enough to be normative for the Constitution itself—like self-directed conduct generally and "government by reflection and choice."[32]

Thought about government's role can begin with three statements we have already discussed, the first by Publius and the remaining two by Lincoln. In *Federalist* No. 10 Publius says that "the first object of Government" is "the protection of different and unequal faculties of acquiring property" (10:58). To Congress on July 4, 1861, Lincoln said that "the free institutions we enjoy have developed the powers and improved the conditions of our whole people, beyond any example in the world." And in the same speech Lincoln said that America's is a "government whose leading object is to elevate the condition of men; to lift artificial weight from all shoulders; to clear the paths of laudable pursuit for all; to afford all an unfettered start and a fair chance in the race of life."[33] Publius thus refers to government's *protecting* faculties that Lincoln has government *developing* in addition to protecting. These statements can easily serve as a framework for policy aims that Nussbaum derives from Aristotle's theory of the basic capabilities that constitute human well-being. These policy aims include "comprehensive health care" (at least for children just starting life's race, I would add); "security of life and property" and "protection from assaults and other preventable pain"; "a humanistic form of education" that is allied with "protection of the arts" and includes "education and training of many kinds" that foster the capacity of citizens "to regulate . . . by their own practical reason and choice" their nutrition, housing, medical treatment, and sexual activity; "support for rich social relations with others" (like marriage); policies "promoting due respect for other species of the world," along with "healthy air and water"; policies that promote "recreational facilities and forms of labor that permit the choice of recreation and enjoyment"; and "protection of a sphere of noninterference around the person . . . so that, according to practical reason and in relationship with others, each person can choose, in his or her own context, to lead his or her very own life."[34]

---

[32] Sunstein, *Partial Constitution*, 136–41. Consider an equivalent view in Mansfield, "The Formal Constitution," 188. Here Mansfield apparently holds that the Constitution "allows the people to choose for itself, to govern itself," and that "the common end" in the debate "over what should be taught in public schools" is "to create independent citizens capable of choosing on their own."

[33] Basler, *Lincoln: His Speeches and Writings*, 606, 607.

[34] Nussbaum, "Aristotelian Social Democracy," 229–30.

Nussbaum emphasizes that objectives like these are, for an Aristotelian, "at least as basic, and perhaps more so than the scheme of offices and concrete judicial and deliberative institutions" (229). These policy aims, in other words, enjoy what we in the present discussion would call *constitutional status*. They, or something like them—something flowing from a persuasive theory of human well-being—are constitutionally obligatory on officials who swear fidelity to the scheme of offices and powers. This conclusion seems no less true for American constitutionalists; because their institutions make sense only as means to policy pursuits of the kind Nussbaum outlines, some such pursuits are at least as obligatory on officials as the institutional rules that define their offices. As Publius says in *Federalist* No. 45, no institutional scheme has any value other than as it may serve the people's welfare. There seems no reason why this should exclude the welfare of the poor. Diamond, another Aristotelian, understood Publius to include the faculties of everyone in his statement about protecting the faculties for acquiring property, the faculties both of "the little . . . and of the much propertied."[35] If protecting the natural faculties of the little propertied in ways that make them "sanguine about their chances" (650) should require food, housing, health care, education of the young, and restraints on the power of corporate wealth in the labor market, and if these things do not happen without government, then government is obligated to do what it can.

The picture sketched here is offered only as an example of a substantive conception of the general welfare that fits the relevant legal-cultural material and claims some measure of independent attractiveness. Though it may do neither of these things as well as rival conceptions, it can at least start a conversation and direct it away from conceptions of the general welfare that will not work. Among these ineligible conceptions are those that deliberately elevate doctrines of religious, racial, or sexual supremacy to the level of political principle. One can acknowledge the racist, sexist, and sectarian strains of political belief in America while recognizing the legal and cultural forces arrayed against racism, sexism, and sectarianism *as self-conscious constitutional commitments*. Describing the system as racist, sexist, or sectarian usually connotes criticism and occasions denials and quests for justifications of the system whose appeal reaches across racial, gender, and sectarian lines. If no such account exists—or, equivalently, if there is no sufficiently strong residual identity (or self) detachable from racial, gender, or sectarian characteristics, or if "government by reflection and choice" cannot plausibly be seen as an aspiration of humankind as

[35] Diamond, "The Federalist," 650.

such, or if some plausible account of the American way fails as a reasonable approximation of that aspiration—then the Constitution is a
mistake. Avoiding this conclusion can be seen as a motivation of recent
works that defend classical rationalism and the quest for truth in science and ethics and link that possibility to constitutional aspirations.[36]

Competing conceptions of the general welfare include those forms
of utilitarianism that conceive the community's well-being as some aggregate of subjective satisfactions such that "[t]he man with many wid-
gets [or dollars for groceries] may place so much more value on them
than the man with only a few that a move of only one unit toward
equality would in fact reduce total satisfaction."[37] Conceptions of this
kind are vulnerable to the textualist objection that they can guarantee
only what Charles Black referred to as "the *partial* welfare," not the
general welfare.[38] As versions of the general welfare they stand or fall
on the strength of arguments for and against subjective forms of utilitarianism. These theories seem implausible, as we have seen, because
they ignore the fallibility of perception and because they admit results
that conflict with the considered judgments of ordinary moral experience. They find it difficult to explain, for example, the ordinary sense
that greed is a vice or the ordinary aversion to the prospect of living
as a brain that Robert Nozick imagined in the vat of an "experience
machine" that would give each brain whatever illusion it desired, or
the ordinary judgment that the state is not obligated to show equal
concern and respect for the preferences or desires of sadists and other
psychopaths.[39]

Conflicts with ordinary experience hardly disprove philosophic arguments, for the experiences in question are laden with beliefs that
may be mistaken. But the deeper structural features of ordinary beliefs,
moral and nonmoral, play a strong role in constitutional thought because ultimate public acceptance is a necessary condition for the legitimacy of any constitutional doctrine, as it is for the Constitution itself.
This last proposition reflects not only the nation's historical experience
but also the language and logic of the constitutional document. The
document is written in the first-person plural, a preambulatory "We"
that includes a founding generation and its "Posterity." The "We" de-

---

[36] See Barber, *Constitution of Judicial Power*, chap. 6; Thomas L. Pangle, *The Spirit of
Modern Republicanism* (Chicago: University of Chicago Press, 1988), 4, 12, 124–27, 252–68,
276–79; Stephen G. Salkever, *Finding the Mean: Theory and Practice in Aristotelian Political
Philosophy* (Princeton, N.J.: Princeton University Press, 1990), chaps. 1, 6.

[37] Winter, "Poverty, Economic Equality, and the Equal Protection Clause," 63.

[38] Black, "Further Reflections on the Constitutional Justice of Livelihood," 1106–7; see
also Edelman, "The Next Century of Our Constitution," 31.

[39] See Brink, *Moral Realism and the Foundations of Ethics*, 223–31.

clares "supreme Law" this set of institutional arrangements, powers, and exemptions conceived as both instrumental to and, once declared supreme law, partially constitutive of purposes like "Justice," "domestic Tranquility," and "the general Welfare." Individual members of this "We" agree in advance to this government's control of such of their private conduct as conflicts with the public ends in view. The well-being of these members must therefore be conceived as not incompatible with the public ends in view.

The Constitution's voice is thus a voice inside the presuppositions that define ordinary moral and nonmoral experience. Subjectivist forms of utilitarianism deviate from the conventional appeals to public purposes—and thus to larger selves—that have always been salient in constitutional language and discussion in America. Should they prove true philosophically *despite* everyday moral intuitions, the Constitution and its discourse will have proved to be mistakes. Falling with preference utilitarianism and for the same reason are social Darwinism and any form of free-market ideology that defines the general welfare as whatever an unregulated market might happen to bring about.

Chapter Six

IS THE CONSTITUTION ADEQUATE TO ITS ENDS?

FROM the hypothesis regarding individual and social well-being set forth in the last chapter, the Constitution's adequacy is a broad question of whether the nation can reasonably expect progress or arguable progress against problems like racism, the income gap, and the degraded economic and social conditions of several rural and urban underclasses. Constitutional theory can show, as I have tried to do here, why and how such policy concerns are connected to the Constitution. But constitutional theory is a relatively self-contained enterprise only when addressing such questions as the Constitution's relationship to the general welfare, the constitutionally embodied conception of the general welfare, which institutions are authorized to do what sorts of things in pursuit of the general welfare, and whether specific kinds of efforts violate specific institutional prerogatives (e.g., of the several states) or individual rights (e.g., to compensation for wealth transfers as "takings" of private property for "public use"). When observers, official or academic, apply constitutional principles to government's responses to actual social conditions, constitutional theorists must depend on answers to scientific questions that are beyond the scope of constitutional theory. The scope and breadth of these questions along any presumed dimension of well-being can be daunting. Regarding poverty alone, for example, issues beyond constitutional theory include questions of who and how many are poor, the kinds and causes of poverty, its economic geography, what it will take to cure the curable kinds, what kinds of programs lead to chronic dependency, public perception of the poor, the extent and structure of public support for poverty relief, and many others.

This dependence on scientific findings in highly disputed areas of economics and social behavior restricts constitutional theory to mere hypothetical assessments of actual institutional prospects. One might contend, for example, that *if* (as seems to me) middle- and upper-class and mostly white America is unwilling to support the programs in family services, housing, education, and public-works employment that seem necessary in this period of global technological advance to give reasonable hope of economic integration to a significant part of black America, and *if* (as I also believe) the nation can afford these investments, then government in America will not approximate what constitutional theory firmly discloses to be the Constitution's promise of equal political and economic opportunity for all and an adequate level of material well-being for every child and every adult who is or was willing to make what Lawrence Sager calls "reasonable efforts in their own behalf."[1] This governmental failure would be also a constitutional failure if it reflected a structural property of the Constitution, as I think it clearly does. In normal times the electorate prefers relatively short-range private purposes to public purposes; hence the failure seriously to pursue a regime of equal opportunity. This failure belies the framers' conviction that the nation could pursue the common good not through cultivating civic virtue but through artfully arranged private incentives.[2] For this reason alone, and in this respect, the Constitution may well be inadequate to the general welfare.

WELFARE AND POWER: STRUCTURE AND CONTEXT OF THE QUESTION

The Constitution's adequacy to any conception of the general welfare depends, as a formal matter, on issues of *power, institutional competence*, and *rights*. The question of power divides broadly into two kinds that reflect a distinction between government through penalties and government through incentives: whether the national government can lawfully use its powers to tax and spend to pursue its version of the general welfare in relatively indirect and noncoercive ways, and whether immediately coercive power for the same purpose is authorized by the commerce clause, the enforcement provisions of the Civil War amendments, and other grants of regulatory power. The question of rights involves issues of two broad kinds: one kind affects the (claimed) rights of the immediate beneficiaries of the welfare provision in question (police protection, educational opportunity, food stamps, etc.); the other kind affects the (claimed) rights of those from whom the government extracts the immediate resources (taxpayers' money, conscripted manpower, the natural freedom to benefit one's self through violence and in other criminalized ways). Thus it can be asked whether duly enacted welfare provision for the poor violates the economic rights of the affluent by imposing either taxes or use regulations that amount to uncompensated takings of private property for public use or deprivations of property without due process of law, both forbidden by the Fifth and Fourteenth Amendments. For their part, the

---

[1] See Sager, "Justice in Plain Clothes," 411, 420.
[2] Barber, *Constitution of Judicial Power*, 113, 235–36.

immediate beneficiaries might ask, with Judge Winter, whether the government's provision of in-kind benefits or conditioned benefits (receipt conditioned on staying in school, keeping a job, noncohabitation, etc.) diminishes their personal liberty by paternalistic imposition and by diversion of resources from the private production of what would otherwise be a larger array of consumer options. The questions of institutional competence divide into two types: one involves which level of government, federal or state, is responsible for what specific kinds of welfare provision; the other involves the respective roles of the judicial and legislative branches in specific kinds of welfare provision.

The broad conception of "welfare" defended in chapter 1 on grounds of fairness thus proves to be something of an analytic liability: it turns the Constitution's formal adequacy to the general welfare into a puzzle that compounds the philosophic issues with the legal issues of federalism, the separation of powers, and individual rights—issues that change, or could change, from one kind of benefit to the next, even if one benefit (like equal opportunity, a national responsibility, arguably) is impossible without another (like an adequate education, a duty some say is left to the several states). The task is further complicated by centuries of judicial doctrine that is still evolving, some of it (as *DeShaney* proves) in wrong directions. Because this book is something of a prolegomenon to the legal issues, submitted in hopes of orienting a discussion it would stimulate, this concluding chapter cannot exhaust the legal issues regarding welfare. Borrowing from arguments I have made elsewhere, I offer here a summary treatment of the pivotal issue: Congress's power vis-á-vis the powers of the several states. I also try to show how principles of the instrumental constitution should orient analysis of, and bias the answers to, the questions I leave to other writers.

What makes Congress's power the pivotal issue is a point to be emphasized before any discussion of the legal specifics: *the general welfare is an end of government—it is a provision of power, not an exemption from power.* This proposition implicates legislative more than judicial power, public attitudes more than negative constitutional restraints. It presupposes a public whose opinions are so structured that it can fairly be described as one that sees the Constitution as an expression of its aspirations—a population whose members see themselves (or can be brought to see themselves) as the "We" of the "We the People." It presupposes civic virtue whose specific content is reflected in the Constitution's means and ends: a deliberative and self-critical concern for achieving a good state of affairs for all, with goodness conceived in terms of preambulatory public purposes like "Justice" and "the general Welfare."[3]

This view of the Constitution need not be utopian in a strong sense because it need not require that all or even most of the public display the requisite concerns in a public-spirited way. It requires only that some do and that those who do enjoy political power by virtue either of the public's considered trust or of the opportunities for public-spirited leadership created by the public's divisions and private preoccupations.[4] Nor does it require a consensus on the best way to achieve constitutional ends—just the opposite, in fact. Again I emphasize this old point, borrowed from Ronald Dworkin, and reformulated in moral realist terms: A concern for the general well-being is a concern for what must be thought the real thing. It is not a concern for one's opinion of the real thing, qua one's opinion; that would be a concern for self, its assertion a form of self-assertion. Genuine concern for the general welfare must therefore involve parties who are open to the criticism of others who may have better evidence and better arguments; it must involve good-faith disagreements and temporary victories for what all sides can appreciate as at least reasonable, if defective, versions of the real thing.[5] Though agreement is a sign of truth because disagreement presupposes answers that are demonstrably right to reasonable and

[3] Barber, *On What the Constitution Means*, 105–15.

[4] See Sunstein, *Partial Constitution*, 20–22. I do not minimize the concern with reelection that political scientists have long found to be uppermost in the minds of elected politicians. I note only the claim to public-spiritedness that pervades the rhetoric of elected politicians and that is integral to the case they make for themselves to the voters. There seems no successful way to deny that this claim is at least a dimension of their self-understanding and therewith a dimension of an empirical reality. By the moral metaphysics of everyday life, at any rate, the claim to public-spiritedness can be either approximately true or false in a given case or among the politicians of a given culture generally. The Constitution's adequacy to the general welfare depends partly on this claim to public-spiritedness being true most of the time and seen by the public to be true most of the time. Skeptics about the very possibility of truth-value in these claims have no contribution to make to the questions of this book or to any normative discussion. Skeptics about the claims of American politicians do have something to say here: they condemn America's political culture and formal constitution as inadequate to constitutional ends. This last form of skepticism hardly condemns constitutional principles; it can take them to be obligatory. It is compatible with and concomitant to the activities of constitution making and constitutional reform. Publius showed this by example when he criticized most politicians (most politicians being state and local politicians), the constitution (the Articles of Confederation), and the public philosophy (the small-republic ideology) of his day.

[5] See Dworkin, *Taking Rights Seriously*, 134–35; Barber, *On What the Constitution Means*, 116–21, 141–44.

competent parties in full possession of the evidence, and though evidence should be sought and agreement pursued, disagreement is both the impetus to and the context of truth-seeking.[6] A population that is perfectly homogeneous and content may be "happy as a clam," but its members will have no opinion of their situation because they have no reason to question it, no reason to bring it to articulate consciousness. These creatures will not be happy in a distinctly human way. The general welfare is an aspiration and a dutiful concern only where conditions favor its pursuit and its meaning is debatable, not where the normative gap between opinion and knowledge is closed. This is why a welfare constitutionalist will value the secular reasonableness, institutionalized self-criticism, reasonable diversity, civil rights and liberties, equal opportunity, and economic promise of a liberal order.

The Constitution's Formal Adequacy

We have seen that the Constitution's formal adequacy to the general welfare is chiefly a question of constitutional power. Following Diamond, Storing, and Berns, I have shown how constitutional rights and structures help to define the ends that government is authorized to pursue. The Civil War amendments and the Bill of Rights, now nationalized, combine to preclude the enactment into law of (overtly) racist and religious views of the general welfare. Rights secured by these provisions are consistent with the state's pursuing a bourgeois view: wellbeing as the psychological and intellectual capacity for effective choice among ways of life that contribute to the pursuit and enjoyment of material security and comfort, bodily health and longevity, and scientific and technological progress, with progress conceived in terms of relieving toil and earthly insecurities. These rights also leave a place for nonviolent forms of antiliberalism and nonliberalism—religious, ideological, artistic, and philosophic. The same holds for constitutional structures. Construed with constitutional rights, the Constitution's guarantee of republican governments in the states (Art. IV, sec. 4) and its prohibiting titles of nobility and religious tests for office (Art. I, sec. 9, and Art. IV, sec. 3, respectively) all elevate the interests of bourgeois liberalism (Mansfield's "interests that can be represented")[7] over the claims of monarchy (whether by God's grace or by natural inheritance)

---

[6] For the demonstrability of right answers, see Moore, "Metaphysics, Epistemology, and Legal Theory," 475–83. For the dependence of truth-seeking on contexts of disagreement, see Barber, *Constitution of Judicial Power*, 265–66 n. 5.

[7] Mansfield, "Hobbes and the Science of Indirect Government," 107.

and aristocracy (either inherited or deserved by standards beyond popular approval). Our question is whether the Constitution grants Congress the power to promote the general welfare as conceived by bourgeois liberalism—to promote, that is, the capacity of each competent person to choose among and participate in either the laudable or the nonviolent pursuits of a liberal order.

At some level such a power would be hard to deny because the Preamble expressly promises no more than power *to promote* the general welfare, and promoting some result can fall far short of pursuing it to the fullest. If no more than promoting were involved, then Congress could fulfill that promise if it had no more than power over post offices and post roads: Congress could exercise that power for limited contributions to those dimensions of human well-being (capacities for friendship, the pursuit of knowledge, etc.) that involve the use of post offices and post roads. More is obviously involved, however, because the powers of Congress are numerous and far from modest. Article I, section 8, and the enforcement provisions of the Civil War amendments give Congress *some* power in areas ranging from the nation's internal and external commerce, war and peace with other nations, and the race relations of the country. Though finite, this list of authorizations includes, most interestingly for our purposes, the power to tax and spend for the general welfare. Yet the very enumeration of Congress's powers and the reservation in the Tenth Amendment of other powers to the states and to the people imply limits on Congress's authorized ends beyond the limits associated with the rights of individuals and structural principles like the separation of powers and the composition of Congress. So our question is not whether Congress can consult the general welfare in using what powers it has. Assuming that the Constitution envisions a conception of the general welfare and that Congress has a constitutional duty to do what it legally can to promote that conception, we now ask whether Congress can lawfully do whatever it takes to promote that conception.

The answer seems initially to be no for two reasons, only one of which survives further reflection. First, as we have seen, the Constitution itself precludes certain antiliberal conceptions of the general welfare. If the arguments for those conceptions should somehow prove stronger than the arguments for conceptions that fit constitutional rights and structures, the Constitution is simply inadequate to its ends. A constitution fully adequate to any end conceived independently of its own operation—justice, national security, the people's welfare, and so forth—would contain no restriction on its choice of means. This includes restrictions derived from structural rules, the very rules that constitute the government and serve partially as the basis for the public's distinguishing lawful government from other entities. No rule-constituted entity can be fully and finally adequate to the general welfare itself. And since the Constitution establishes a rule-constituted entity, the Constitution's adequacy can be no more than relative and provisional.[8] Constitutional adequacy depends on the conjunction of two contingencies: (1) the approximate soundness of the case for constitutionally governed bourgeois liberalism as a good way of life under foreseeable conditions and in view of the alternative regimes and the costs of change, and (2) the persuasiveness of that case to the general public.

As we saw when analyzing Publius's theory of responsible government in chapter 2, the Constitution designs its government for an educative function; at its best, constitutional government reconciles public opinion to reasonable approximations of what is right and good. Constitutional government reconciles public opinion to the people's well-being—that is, to what can stand independently of public opinion as a defensible approximation of the people's well-being. The Constitution succeeds or fails to the extent that the government it establishes can lead the public toward an objective approximation of the people's well-being. This need for the convergence of subjective and objective well-being makes subjective well-being a necessary condition for the Constitution's success. A decline in subjective well-being can thus indicate constitutional failure. Though this observation is complicated by the fallibility of perceived wants and the way expectations influence impressions of well-being, the Constitution's electoral provisions imply that subjective awareness is an element of well-being. This is why constitutionalists cannot afford to ignore recent findings of a general loss of happiness in market democracies.[9]

Even if our bourgeois liberalism should prove both sound and popular relative to alternative ways of life, the Constitution might still be inadequate to the general welfare. Constitutionally granted powers may fall short even of a constitutional conception of well-being. This brings us to the second reason for doubting the Constitution's adequacy. This reason flows partly from the nature of well-being and partly from the nature of Congress's power. I have assumed here arguendo that the general welfare is the welfare of every responsible person, and following Nussbaum (who follows Aristotle in a way that resonates with liberal statesmen like Publius and Lincoln) I have hypothesized that persons do not fare well merely because they possess property or actually enjoy certain relationships; they fare well if they

---

[8] See Barber, *On What the Constitution Means*, 45–61.
[9] Lane, *Loss of Happiness in Market Democracies*, esp. chaps 1, 5–6.

exercise the psychological and intellectual faculties or capacities to acquire or enjoy what they reasonably want by way of property, relationships, vocations, and avocations. These faculties and capacities are developed in our culture by educational institutions like the family and the public schools or state-licensed and state-facilitated private schools. And it is this dependence of well-being on these educational institutions that seems to disable the government established by the Constitution.

Constitutional tradition in America denies Congress direct power over education of the nation's youth (other than military personnel and residents of the territories and the nation's capital). Though the Constitution does not expressly say so, responsibility for educating the young is usually said to be reserved to the states. True, the Supreme Court has held that states that elect to operate public schools cannot do so in ways that offend proscriptions like the establishment clause and the equal protection clause. But the Court has also held, in effect, that the Constitution does not compel the states either to establish schools de novo or to maintain educational systems once established.[10] And by the traditional understanding of its enumerated powers, Congress cannot act on its own if the states choose to leave education to some consortium of "the market" and "the family"—even if this results in systems of "private schools" determined to inculcate sectarian or racist beliefs and attitudes that are fatal to liberal constitutionalism. Thus, observers can doubt that Congress can legitimately use its granted powers to foster a liberal culture in the nation's schools or to oppose those attitudes (racism, social Darwinism, antiscientific and antiliberal religiosity) that effectively limit the social, economic, and political opportunities of some of the nation's people.

I accept the first argument for the Constitution's inadequacy. There is of course a rich tradition of criticizing bourgeois liberalism that stretches from Rousseau and the Anti-federalists to John Paul II, with Marx, Nietzsche, Strauss, Arendt, King, and Sandel along the way. In view of this many-faceted criticism, the Constitution's adequacy must be treated as an open question. But the mere fact of the criticism is hardly enough to close the question. Mere disagreement over the Constitution's adequacy cannot establish the Constitution's inadequacy because a political aspiration like the people's welfare presupposes a public debate about its content and rational pursuit. Disagreement about these matters is both the medium and the instrument for pursuing the general welfare as a real value. What does make the Constitution inadequate is a defect of all rule-constituted instruments: they can-

[10] See *San Antonio v. Rodriguez*, 411 U.S. 1, 33–35 (1973).

not avoid committing themselves to conceptions whose attractiveness is contingent on historical conditions beyond human control. The Constitution's adequacy is thus wholly contingent on how the case for bourgeois liberalism continues to fare against evidence continually marshaled against it. Because this ever-changing evidence flows from and reflects unpredictable natural and social change, judgments of the Constitution's adequacy can never amount to more than qualified, relative, and provisional affirmations of continuing political efforts to cope with continuing challenges.[11] Few will deny this proposition in an age of global terrorism, global markets, and global warming, each a grave challenge that the constitutional order may well fail to meet.

But the second reason for denying the Constitution's adequacy is harder to accept. I refer to the states' rights challenge to the Constitution's adequacy. It holds that the reserved powers of the states disable Congress from doing all that a government could successfully do to promote any conception of the good life, including a bourgeois conception of the good life. A committed states' righter questions any reference to a "national community" in America.[12] She would oppose federal reform of the nation's schools, even when their performance was hurting the nation's economy and military readiness.[13] This states' rights position is untenable because it flows from what is at best a debatable treatment of historical material and the rejection of a moral position that is hard to oppose. On the historical question, the states' rights position is burdened by an undeniable historical fact: the impetus for the Constitution had little if anything to do with preserving the prerogatives of the states. Suzette Hemberger puts is well: "The Philadelphia Convention was called by those who believed it was necessary to strengthen the national govenment; those who did not share this belief stayed home. Debates within the Convention were, for the most part, debates among nationalists."[14] States' rights did not need a new constitution; they did well enough under the Articles of Confederation, and the states' rights party lost at ratification. The Constitution

[11] The implications of this proposition for the theory of political obligation under the Constitution are developed in Barber, *On What the Constitution Means*, chap. 3.

[12] See William A. Schambra, "Progressive Liberalism and American 'Community,' " *The Public Interest*, no. 8 (summer 1985): 38–42, 46–48.

[13] See James Jackson Kilpatrick, "The Case for States' Rights," in Goldwin, ed., *A Nation of States*, 103–4 (criticizing the National Defense Education Act of 1958 as a step toward federal control "of what shall be taught, and to whom, and by whom, and in what sort of buildings").

[14] Suzette Hemberger, "What Did They Think They Were Doing When They Wrote the U.S. Constitution, and Why Should We Care?" in Barber and George, eds., *Constitutional Politics*, 128.

originated, for better or worse, in concerns about territorial disputes among the states, an unpaid war debt, declining investor confidence, threats of debtor insurrection, barriers to interstate trade, and the failure of foreign states to honor treaties with the United States.[15] These problems would not have been seen as problems by people who had no sense of themselves as members of a national community and no sense of government as dedicated to ends like national security, honor, and prosperity. So the Preamble turns out fairly to reflect a historical fact: while it numbers a "more perfect Union" among the ends of the government it establishes, it says nothing about the rights of the states.

For the other side it can be said, however, that the campaign for ratification would have failed had the Constitution's supporters not promised a bill of rights, and that the Bill of Rights that was eventually ratified contains the Tenth Amendment. Furthermore, the Tenth Amendment was prefigured by the repeated assurances of *The Federalist* that the concerns of the proposed government were relatively few (see 14:86; 17:107–8; 33:204–8; 39:254, 256; 45:310–13; 51:351). By forcing these concessions on the Federalists, the Anti-Federalists helped shape the Constitution and thus earned the right to be numbered among its framers. No less a nationalist than Herbert Storing acknowledged as much.[16] This claim for the Anti-Federalists derives further support from Jefferson's election in 1800. Treating the author of the Declaration of Independence as something less than a "founding father" would condemn that designation as capricious, and Jefferson with the latter Madison, both of them framers, forged a states' rights view of the Constitution that survives to the present as a force in American politics. All this supports Storing's assessment of the nation's political life as "a dialogue, in which the Anti-Federalist concerns and principles still play an important part."[17]

But the most that this last observation could establish is that the historical record is mixed as between nationalist and state's rights views of the American founding. And if the record is mixed, a normative conception of the founding as either predominantly nationalist or confederal needs, even among originalists, something more than the citation of historical material. When constitutional text and history fail to communicate a uniform message, an ethical argument is needed for reading text and history one way rather than another. This need for an ethical argument is sufficient to favor a nationalist view because an ethical argument must seek one (or one set) as opposed to a plurality

---

[15] See *The Federalist*, 6:37–43.
[16] Storing, *What the Anti-Federalists* Were For, 3.
[17] Ibid.

of conflicting normative standards. The good or the right that would recommend a states' rights view in the dialogue Storing describes would have to be a value that holds for the nation as a whole. But a value that holds for the nation as a whole would be a controlling national value, precisely something whose existence the states' rights position implicitly denies. If states' righters proposed to their nationalist interlocutors that either justice or happiness or the ennobling effects of civic autonomy favor states rights,[18] they would have to refer to more than mere local versions of justice or happiness or nobility or civic autonomy. The nature of these values would then determine the meaning and the extent of the states' rights favored, and that determination would be left to persons acting as agents of the nation. If the states' existence were justified by, say, the greater opportunity they afforded for civic participation, the nation's courts would decide what "civic participation" requires and whether it permits the exclusion of some minority. The dialogue to which Storing referred must perforce be a national dialogue appealing to a nationalist sense in quest of national norms.[19] Such is the inherent weakness of any states' rights view of the Constitution. States' rights makes more sense as a base for opposing the Constitution than for interpreting it.

The moral case against any strong states' rights view of national power to promote the general welfare is the one Madison makes in *Federalist* No. 45: No form of government whatever has any other value than as it may be fitted to pursue the people's welfare. To this Madison adds that concern for states' rights at the expense of the people's welfare revives "in another shape" the old-world doctrine "that the people were made for kings," not kings for the "peace, liberty, and safety" of the people (45:309). Here Madison assumes that peace, liberty, and safety are more conducive to the people's welfare than the virtues presupposed by, and cultivated through, participation in smaller governmental units that enjoy real power to pursue, without leave of higher authority, conceptions of the good (nobility, God-fearing righteousness, racial integrity, cultural refinement) that subordinate bourgeois peace, liberty, and safety. But Madison's point in *Federalist* No. 45 centers not on his substantive assumptions about the good life. He is arguing about the relationship between two types of consideration: what makes for happiness, and what powers government should (be construed to)

---

[18] See Harvey C. Mansfield and Delba Winthrop, "Liberalism and Big Government: Tocqueville's Analysis," in Melzer et al., eds., *Politics at the Turn of the Century*, 110–12.

[19] For a parallel argument to the effect that a states' righter's reliance on the Tenth Amendment implicitly concedes the right of a national institution (the Supreme Court) to decide, see Berns, "The Meaning of the Tenth Amendment," 130–31.

have. He is saying that the question of happiness comes first and governs the question of power. Thus he adds that if his own constitutional plan were "adverse to the public happiness," his advice would be to "reject the plan." And if "the Union itself" were "inconsistent with the public happiness," he would advise: "abolish the Union" (309).

Who is left to debate this position? Where is the organized political party of any electoral significance, national or regional, that is serious about letting the states pursue their own distinctive versions of the good, whatever they might turn out to be? In asking this question, I put aside academic multiculturalism and postmodernism for reasons that apply to skepticism generally. First, as forms of academic moral skepticism, radical multiculturalism and postmodernism can do no more than deny the second-order assumptions of any and all moral stances; they cannot support a moral stance of their own.[20] No first-order proposition about the (simple) fairness of X can either follow from or coexist with the second-order proposition that there is no (simple) fairness. If there is no fairness, it cannot be unfair for one person or one community to impose its view of fairness on another. Second, everyday moral stances and ordinary life generally presuppose a moral reality. To say that imposition is unfair is to say that imposition is objectively unfair. Third, the concrete moral stance presupposes a normative gap between opinion and truth, belief and reality. With the normative gap come the two additional assumptions that the speaker is fallible and that willful imposition on other competent persons is wrong. These additional assumptions prepare the speaker to value philosophic quest and its preconditions, like the moral equality of interlocutors as such, the right of each freely to opine without fear of reprisal, and the duty of each to give and to consider nonprivileged evidence and to follow the argument wherever it leads.[21]

Finally, though I am as concerned about the nation's divisions as anyone, I note the current inability of the Religious Right to achieve credible third-party status and its willingness to settle for a muted (if powerful) voice within the Republican Party, the decline of violent groups on both the left and the right, and the willingness even of admitted sectarians to offer clearly secular arguments for their positions on matters like abortion and euthanasia.[22] These factors strengthen recent sociological findings that the nation is not as divided as postmod-

---

[20] Brian Barry exposes the normative incapacity of contemporary multiculturalism in his *Culture and Equality* (Cambridge: Harvard University Press, 2001), chap 7.

[21] Barber, *Constitution of Judicial Power*, 191–97, 201, 214, 232–34.

[22] See, e.g., Gerard V. Bradley, "*Life's Dominion*: A Review Essay," *Notre Dame Law Review* 69 (1993): 329, esp. 366–68, 374–80; John Finnis, "The Rights and Wrongs of Abortion," *Philosophy and Public Affairs* 2 (1973): 117; George, "Justice, Legitimacy, and Alle-

ernist projections on reality might suggest.[23] All but a relatively few Americans still seem willing to talk to each other about divisive matters. And so I ask again: Where is the party with any electoral significance—where, indeed, is the organized faction of any significant party—that is willing to let the several states do whatever their thing might be in matters such as education, marriage, public morals, and homeland security, all of these arguably beyond what the framers clearly expected to be Congress's concerns?

No party argues today for repealing the First Amendment (or overruling its application to the states) and permitting the establishment of Christian commonwealths in states that want them. No party argues for letting these states decide to bar women from higher education or careers outside the home, if that is what they want to do. No party claims the states have reserved power to stone adulterers, Taliban style, if that is what their people are destined to want. No party contends that a correct view of the Constitution permits the states to forbid interracial education and marriage. Cultural conservatives in the U.S. Senate abandoned a states' rights reading of Congress's power under the Fourteenth Amendment when they sought to disarm *Roe v. Wade* with the Human Life Bill of 1981, which would have protected the fetus as a person.[24] Congressional conservatives did the same when they supported the Religious Freedom Restoration Act of 1993.[25] Conservatives in Congress did not leave education, health, and sexual morality to the states when they amended the Welfare Reform Act of 1996 to provide federal funds for state sex-education programs that stress abstinence before marriage, barring those funds to programs (favored by some 80 percent of parents polled nationally) that encourage use of condoms or contraception among sexually active teens.[26] Economic conservatives routinely disregard states' rights when their interests are in question, as is evident in calls for Congress to cap damage awards in civil suits against corporations under state law and for the federal courts to grant compensation (under an incorporated right) for property owners facing state land-use regulations. Instead of telling the Boy Scouts of America they could vote with their feet simply by disbanding

giance," 319–20; Germain Grisez, "When Do People Begin?" *Proceedings of the American Catholic Philosophic Association* 53 (1990): 27–47.

[23] See Alan Wolfe, *One Nation after All* (New York: Penguin Books, 1998), esp. 61–81.

[24] See U.S. Senate, Subcommittee on Separation of Powers, *The Human Life Bill: Hearings on S. 158*, 97th Cong., 1st sess. (1981); *Roe v. Wade* (1973).

[25] The Supreme Court voided the act in *Boerne v. Flores*, 521 U.S. 507 (1997). For comment on the act's offense to federalism, see Eisgruber and Sager, "Why the Religious Freedom Restoration Act Is Unconstitutional," 464–67.

[26] *New York Times*, December 28, 2000, A1.

in New Jersey, five erstwhile states' righters on the Supreme Court recently reshaped doctrine regarding the First Amendment (another incorporated right) and denied the states power to open the Boy Scouts to homosexuals.[27] The same five later reshaped equal-protection doctrine to invalidate Florida's standard for counting ballots in a presidential election.[28] And, at this writing, conservativess in Congress propose a national law against partial-birth abortions under the commerce clause that will override the policies of some states.[29] Because, therefore, the American Right regularly joins the American Left in honoring only those state policies that conform to their views of what national standards ought to be, both sides treat active citizenship in, and associated virtues of, local and regional republican units as goods that are subordinate to what they see as the constitutional ends and standards of a continental democracy.

Refuting Publius's moral claim (constitutional form takes its value from service to the people's welfare) would take a complex argument. That argument would have to contend, first, that man-made constitutional forms can be understood with no reference either to the people's welfare in general or to any specific substantive goods as good in themselves. It would have to contend further that the only real good is a will disposed to do what is morally right. And it would have to prove, finally, that a states' rights reading of the Constitution is compulsory for a good will. No such argument has been made, and until it is, text, history, and common sense combine to justify an instrumentalist reading of Congress's power, as in *The Federalist*, and John Marshall's opinion in *McCulloch v. Maryland*, which still survives the subversion of the Rehnquist Court as our most authoritative statement of state-federal relations.[30]

---

[27] *Boy Scouts of America v. Dale*, 530 U.S. 640 (2000).

[28] *Bush v. Gore*, 531 U.S. 98 (2000).

[29] Partial-Birth Abortion Ban Act of 2002, HR 4965 EH, Sec. 1531 (a), 107th Cong., 2d sess.

[30] Only an instrumentalist argument can defeat the instrumentalist arguments in *McCulloch* and *The Federalist*. It might be said, for example, that the people's welfare depends on the public's believing what only an academic elite knows to be false, namely, that contrary to the *Federalist* No. 45, form *does* have value independently of its service to the people's welfare. This seems to be Mansfield's position in his quarrel with me. Mansfield does not argue against the soundness of arguments like mine, however; he contends only against their publication. Nor is Mansfield's argument chiefly an argument about either welfare or the Constitution. It flows, rather, from his answer to a question about the social obligation of academics: whether or to what extent their obligation to the truth is qualified by their obligation not to disrupt the political arrangements on which their scholarship depends. (See Mansfield, "The Formal Constitution," 187–89; see also Barber, "Reply to Professor Mansfield," 191–94.) I might appreciate Mansfield's

In *McCulloch*, Marshall rejected a negative construction of the necessary and proper clause and a states' rights construction of the Tenth Amendment. Why interpret the necessary and proper clause as a restriction on Congress's power and the Tenth Amendment as an enlargement of the power of the states at Congress's expense when the nation's prosperity and security depend on Congress's power? Why let one state overrule the whole people that Congress represents? Why a construction that restricts the national government and fortifies the states when the supremacy clause (Art. VI) grants supremacy not only to national power but, implicitly, to nationally authorized purposes for whose sake the powers were granted? These were Marshall's questions in *McCulloch*.[31] Why—he implicitly asked (to make instrumental sense of the supremacy clause)—why prefer a states' rights construction when, for reasons given in *The Federalist*, the national government is a better government, both structurally and with regard to the quality of its officials, than the governments of the states?[32] Grant Marshall's premises regarding the instrumental nature of the Constitution, America as a national community, and the qualitative superiority of the national government and his questions are hard to answer.

Federalist No. 45 supplies the fundamental principal of Marshall's argument when it claims the people's welfare "is the supreme object to be pursued" and that "no form of government whatever has any other value than as it may be fitted for the attainment of this object." From a Marshallean view of the Constitution as both instrumental and nationalist, the Supreme Court could easily have affirmed Congress's power under section 5 of the Fourteenth Amendment to regulate private conduct restrictive of the economic, political, and thereby ultimately social freedom of racial and ethnic minorities. Judicial doctrine has long held otherwise, of course, motivated partly by a commitment to states' rights and partly to the expressive autonomy of private associations.[33] The best answer to the states' rights commitment is Publius's answer: states' rights must yield to the people's well-being (45:309).

A more interesting question than Congress's power vis-a-vis state governments is whether any government under the Constitution can

---

position on the duty of scholars if I could appreciate his apparent belief that there is something subversive about the constitutionalism of Lincoln, Marshall, and *The Federalist*, as opposed to the constitutionalism of the Rehnquist Court. This, at any rate, is the subject of a different debate.

[31] For this interpretation of *McCulloch*, see Barber, *On What the Constitution Means*, 77–88.

[32] For Marshall's debt to *The Federalist*, see Robert K. Faulkner, *The Jurisprudence of John Marshall* (Princeton, N.J.: Princeton University Press, 1968), 5–6, 79–96.

[33] Barber, *On What the Constitution Means*, 91–94.

lawfully combat antiliberal practices and attitudes in the community. In the case involving the Boy Scouts, the Rehnquist Court held that the First Amendment freedoms of expression and association barred government from requiring the organization to admit homosexuals.[34] The majority contended in essence that the Boy Scouts sought to teach its youthful members a personal morality that excluded homosexuality and that the mere presence of an uncloseted assistant scoutmaster (there was no question of misconduct) would obfuscate the organization's moral message. The Boy Scouts later decided to exclude professed atheists.[35] These events present a different question. I would approach it in terms of two points I have emphasized in this book.

Although the First Amendment does protect the expressive association of some antiliberals, it combines with other constitutional provisions to restrict the expression of other antiliberals. These disfavored groups include undomesticated antiliberals who insists that their racist, sectarian, sexist, and antihomosexual preferences find expression in the law. Regarding homosexuals, the Court itself held in an earlier case that the Colorado Constitution could not prohibit its state and local lawmakers from protecting them from discrimination.[36] Racial, ethnic, and religious minorities in the state could seek such protection from state and local lawmakers, as could veterans, people with children, and others—including smokers. But homosexuals could not. They could not ask state and local lawmakers for relief from discrimination unless they first persuaded Colorado's electorate to repeal a recent constitutional amendment that barred such relief. Homosexuals were thus forced to work harder than others to improve their lot, and instead of a good reason for this discrimination, the Court found an animus in Colorado against homosexuals that offended the federal-constitutional requirement of public reasonableness. Calling this animus "traditional morality" failed to justify it because changes in the public's understanding had brought that part of the traditional morality into question, and the state offered no good reason to support it.

The Colorado case thus confirms that constitutional provisions discriminate against those whom they burden, leaving the question of whether good reasons support the discrimination. The same holds for the First, Fourteenth, and Fifth Amendments. They discriminate against those whom they burden (undomesticated racists, undomesticated believers, undomesticated antihomosexuals, etc.), leaving us to ask whether good reasons support these discriminations. Absent good

[34] *Boys Scouts of America v. Dale*, 530 U.S. 640, 653–57 (2000).

[35] *New York Times*, November 3, 2002, 1A.

[36] *Romer v. Evans*, 317 U.S. 629 (1996).

reasons for these discriminations, the Constitution lapses into an arbitrary, even tyrannical, expression of bourgeois morality and belies its claims to be an instrument of the general welfare as a real good.

Speaking strictly, the First, Fourteenth, and Fifth Amendments do not discriminate against *persons* who hold disfavored beliefs; they discriminate against the beliefs by foreclosing their expression in the law. If this discrimination is reasonable, the beliefs must be false or apparently false, and demonstrably so —demonstrable in principle, that is, to reasonable persons who presently hold the apparently false beliefs.[37] In the broader constitutional context of quest for real goods, the First, Fourteenth, and Fifth Amendments would thus imply that no competent adult possessed of what appears to be the available evidence and motivated to the truth could believe, for example, that homosexuals or atheists as such are immoral. This constitutional discrimination against apparently false beliefs is also discrimination against persons, but only as theoretical types: persons identified as their beliefs, like John the Antihomosexual or John the Antiatheist. If all that can be said of someone is that he is antihomosexual or antiatheist, then the Constitution discriminates, rightly or wrongly, against that person as a person.

But you can always say more of real persons, and when real persons are called antihomosexual, what is meant is that they are persons who have certain attitudes and beliefs in addition (it can go without saying) to many other attitudes and beliefs. That John's antihomosexuality could never constitute his identity is suggested by the fact that we could sensibly say that John had changed his mind about homosexuals. Here we assume a metaphysical distance between John and at least some of his beliefs. Further evidence for the distance between John and some of his beliefs would be his willingness to question the beliefs, translate them if he can into falsifiable propositions, and abandon them if he either cannot translate them or if better evidence should weigh against them. If John could not separate himself from a belief even to reaffirm it, if he were closed to all his experiences, past and imagined, that might go against the belief, then he would be, as we would revealingly say, consumed by the belief. As a psychological matter John would then be one with his belief. He would be, say, the permanently thoroughgoing antihomosexual or antiatheist, not willing to discuss or compromise his belief for any reason

Discriminating against the belief of such a person, if we could imagine him as a real person, would be tantamount to discriminating against him. And the justifying reason would be that he is so com-

---

[37] See Moore, "Metaphysics, Epistemology, and Legal Theory," 475–83.

pletely closed to the evidence of our experiences and reflections that to accept policy predicated on his belief would be to accept his arbitrary tyranny over us, which we could not rationally do for the same reason that we cannot have a reason for abandoning reason. Undomesticated antiliberals approximate this fictional character by refusing to submit their beliefs to forums of public reasonableness. In this way they bring second-class citizenship on themselves. The Constitution prevents these thoroughgoing antiliberals from expressing their distinguishing preferences in the most authoritative choices of the communities in which they live, for to permit them to express themselves in this way would be to accept tyranny.

The Constitution permits government to compel these antiliberals (through taxation, conscription, and the criminal law) to sacrifice life, liberty, and property to support practices they detest. What justifies this imposition is their freedom to oppose the practices they oppose in forums of public reasonableness, the belief that no one can choose to live without reason, and the belief that in the end all competent persons would prefer a regime of reasons available in principle to all, not just one or a few. After all, you cannot know that I have good evidence or any evidence at all if what I have is not available first to you and ultimately to the many critical others who are needed to confirm what might otherwise be bad evidence.

My second point is continuous with the first: A regime truly committed to the general welfare or to any end conceived as a real good must recognize the need for diverse views in dialectical progress toward the best understanding of those ends. This is why scientific and moral realism tend to favor liberalism and liberalism must secure a place for, and protect the expressive freedom of, antiliberalism. I refer, of course, to *domesticated* antiliberalism—the kind that can live with liberalism and whose political proposals admit of translation into the falsifiable proposition of public dialogue. A liberal regime must make room for antiliberal associations of two domesticated kinds: politically active antiliberalism, whose adherents permit themselves to be taxed and conscripted to support a regime they are trying to change by (what they join liberals in calling) nonviolent means, and apolitical antiliberalism, whose members suffer evil passively from faith in either otherworldly or purely private vindication. The worldly powerlessness of passive antiliberalism should not trouble the faithful because they deny the goods of this world. The relative weakness of political antiliberlism can be overcome if time brings repeal or abandonment of the Constitution's commitment to secular reasonableness. Because this is an essential commitment of the nation's present constitution—a char-

ter of *real* benefits among *fallible* beings—abandoning it would mean
not only a different constitution but a different *kind* of constitution.

The need to secure the expressive autonomy of domesticated antiliberals can be seen as a limit on constitutional power and, indeed, a
threat to the Constitution and to constitutionalism generally, admitting
as it does the possibility of a radically different regime. But the presence of a domesticated and active antiliberalism is also an element of
constitutional power, one that is vital to the Constitution's coherence
and existence as what it claims to be. From the welfarist view of the
Constitution that I have defended here, constitutional power is power
to pursue good results. And from the secular moral realism of ordinary
political life, the goods sought are real, not just apparent.[38] Power adequate to the pursuit of real goods must remain open to better arguments regarding their nature and the means thereto. Security for antiliberal criticism (via judicially enforced rights and society's toleration
of domesticated antiliberalism) is an aspect of the requisite openness.
Security for domesticated antiliberalism is thus an element of constitutional power, and constitutional power is undermined by liberal big-
otry against domesticated antiliberalism.

All this suggests that reform of the Boy Scouts and like organizations
(i.e., social organizations that do not function as for-profit public acco-
modations) should come through noncoercive means, not through the
application of law. This reform could be attempted by anyone, including public officials seeking to exercise moral leadership, editorialists,
teachers, and nongovernmental organizations concerned with the survival of constitutional principles in an age of recrudescing antiliberalism. The effort might begin by showing the Boy Scouts that while the
nation must honor their constitutional right to do so, they are begin-
ning to define themselves in a manner that stands against their country's central constitutional commitment. If they cannot come up with
publicly defensible reasons for their policies—good evidence that homosexuals cannot be moral and that duty to God demands the exclusion of atheists—they risk preparing their young members either for
second-class citizenship or for revolution.

We have seen reason to hold that philosophic realism and secular
public reasonableness are central to liberal constitutionalism, that they
presuppose right answers at least to some moral and scientific question, and that right answers are demonstrable in principle to all who
are equipped, motivated, and permitted to reason aright. This demonstrability of right answers makes agreement important. Though not the
source of truth, agreement among good-faith and competent interlocu-

---

[38] See Barber, *Constitution of Judicial Power*, 193–95, 197–201.

tors can be evidence of truth—defeasible evidence, to be sure, since evidence is belief and belief is not truth, but evidence nonetheless. Because liberal constitutionalism (an institutional expression of secular reasonableness wherever technology permits civilization without slavery and predatory war) is driven to coercion only by necessity, regulatory power (power enforced by criminal and civil penalties) in a constitutional regime needs supplementing by power to govern through incentives. This brings us back to the general welfare clause of Article I, section 8: the commerce clause, the taxing power, and other penalty-backed powers are supplemented by the power to spend for the general welfare. It is this power (as noted earlier in connection with Congress's concern for the sexual morality of the nation's youth) that enables Congress to breach limits on its regulatory power that are alleged to result from the reserved powers of the states.

A liberal reading of the general welfare clause is important to any positive assessment of the Constitution's adequacy to the general welfare. This is so because a liberal reading permits Congress to pursue aspects of the general welfare that, by some accounts, exceed ends authorized by Article I and the Civil War amendments. This is not to agree that a correct view of Congress's regulatory powers would fall short of what is needed. Persuaded by *McCulloch* and *Federalist* No. 45, I see no good reason for less than the most generous construction of Congress's regulatory powers. The commerce clause and Congress's powers over bankruptcy, patents and trademarks, and the monetary system, together with restrictions in Article IV on the power of the states to impair contractual obligations—all point to, make sense in view of, a general economic prosperity as a responsibility of the national government. Lesser included goods like unobstructed interstate trade are intrinsically attractive to professional economists, traffic engineers, and the like, not to the ordinary consumers and producers of the preambulatory "We the People." A reasonable interpretation of the regulatory powers would thus install "economic prosperity" as an end that Congress has some duty to promote—and if some, why not all that it would take?[39] How can one say, for example, that the states are

[39] This in effect was Marshall's question in *McCulloch*, where he found restrictions on power to serve nationally authorized ends not in the reserved powers of the states but in the ends themselves (Congress's motives had to remain nonpretextual), in "the great principles of civil liberties," and in the separation of powers. As I have noted, justification for his construction of the Constitution lies in the view that nationally authorized ends are superior in value to contradictory ends (as per the conditional moral argument for bourgeois liberalism) and the national government is a better instrument for pursuing nationally authorized ends. Classical republicans may oppose a position that separates the well-being of all but a fraction of the people from the ennobling responsibilities

absolutely free to locate their capital cities anywhere within their borders when some sites might conflict with what the Department of Defense, the Energy Department, the Corps of Engineers, or the Environmental Protection Agency might hold to be sites foreclosed by their constituent policy objectives?[40] How can one categorically exclude education from Congress's regulatory power over, say, commerce and the armed forces, if schools are failing to produce a population that can keep up with foreign military and economic competition?[41]

Yet the most generous interpretation of Congress's enumerated powers leaves intact the concept of enumerated powers, and that concept is generally taken to imply *some* powers reserved to the states, even if there is no indefeasible specification of what those powers might be (no indefeasible specification because any categorical practice or aspect of life, like education and sexual morality, can come to obstruct goods like national security and prosperity). One can of course contend that the enumeration of powers and the Tenth Amendment are parts of a long tradition of constitutional mistakes, burdens on the Constitution's general normative coherence that include, arguably and by various accounts, the fugitive slave clause, the electoral college, the composition of the Senate, the first section of the Fourteenth Amendment, the Eighteenth Amendment, the free exercise clause, and the Ninth Amendment. But this is not the place for such an argument. I accept here arguendo the enumeration of powers as a valid constitutional principle. But if the enumeration is valid, Congress's *regulatory* powers (principally the categorical powers listed after the general welfare clause in Article I, section 8, and the enforcement sections of the Civil War amendments) could fall short of adequacy to the general welfare. The regulatory powers would be inadequate at the point at which the states' performance in areas like education and public morals became

---

of political office possessed of real power. But Marshall, like Publius, was more attracted to the case for bourgeois liberalism (see Faulkner, *Jurisprudence of John Marshall*, 20–34). I have conceded that the Constitution's adequacy to the general welfare depends on the moral and scientific case for bourgeois liberalism.

[40] Justice O'Connor asserts that the states have such a right; see her dissent in *Garcia v. Metropolitan Transit Authority*, 469 U.S. 528, 586 (1985). Contrast Justice Lurton's opinion in *Coyle v. Oklahoma*, 221 U.S. 559, 574 (1911), which O'Connor cites as supporting her position. Lurton denies that Congress can dictate the location of a state capital by virtue of Congress's power to admit new states. But Lurton suggests Congress *may* determine the location of a state capital if doing so serves purposes "plainly within" its regulatory powers, like the powers over commerce and relations with the Indian tribes.

[41] For a spirited and now classic defense of Congress's power under such circumstances, see Harry V. Jaffa, "The Case for a Stronger National Government," in Goldwin, ed., *A Nation of States*, 115–25.

generally acknowledged problems for the nation's security and economic health.

Here is where the general welfare clause enters as a supplement to the regulatory powers. The Supreme Court, following Alexander Hamilton, has long construed this clause as a power through which Congress can influence policy in areas thought to be reserved to the states.[42] Against critics of his proposals for a national bank, protection for domestic manufacturers, and federally funded canals and other "internal improvements," Hamilton argued for a liberal construction of Congress's regulatory powers *and* for a construction of the general welfare clause as a power to tax and spend for any project conducive to the people's welfare, whether or not embraced by the enumerated regulatory powers.[43] Though Hamilton's theory or something close to his intended application of it (as distinguished from his formal statement of it) is needed for the Constitution's adequacy to the general welfare, I cannot offer an unqualified defense of Hamilton's theory. Elsewhere I have defended a theory of national power that would demand a mode of review that turns on judgments of Congress's motives. The point, simply put, is that if Congress's powers are powers to pursue associated *ends* or *purposes*, observers have to form judgments about Congress's motives to describe what Congress is doing and thus to determine whether it is doing what it is authorized to do.[44] By this theory Congress is limited to authorized purposes regardless of whether it chooses a strategy of penalties or a strategy of incentives.

This purposive theory of congressional power bears formal resemblance to the theory of the general welfare clause favored by James Madison. Though Madison's precise theory is a matter of dispute,[45] he seemed to hold that Congress can tax and spend for authorized purposes only *and* that those purposes were limited to those "within the enumerated authorities vested in Congress," that is, "within" the pow-

---

[42] See *U.S. v. Butler*, 297 U.S. 1 (1936); *Steward Machine Co. v. Davis*, 301 U.S. 548 (1937); *Helvering v. Davis*, 301 U.S. 619 (1937). At this writing, Hamilton's theory of the general welfare clause has apparently survived the Supreme Court's current states' rights revival; see *New York v. U.S.*, 505 U.S. 144, 166–67 (1992); and *Printz v. U.S.*, 521 U.S. 898, at 910–11, 917–18, 936 (1997).

[43] See C. Herman Pritchett, *The American Constitution* (New York: McGraw-Hill, 1968), 245–46.

[44] See Barber, *On What the Constitution Means*, 88–91.

[45] For a recent treatment of the issues, and an attempt to save Madison from the conventional view that he held different views about the general welfare clause at different points in his career, see Leonard R. Sorenson, *Madison and the "General Welfare" of America: His Consistent Constitutional Vision* (Lanham, Md.: Rowman and Littlefield, 1995), esp. chaps. 1, 4, 7.

ers that follow the general welfare clause in Article I, section 8.[46] Madison himself varied in his application of his theory. As president in 1817, he acknowledged the "signal advantage to the general prosperity" of improved roads, canals, and waterways. Yet he held that the power to fund such projects was not "expressly given by the Constitution" and could not "be deduced" from the specific provisions of Article I, section 8, without an "inadmissible latitude of construction."[47] He thus implied that the powers that follow the general welfare clause do not establish "the general prosperity" as a constitutional end that would then justify a policy of internal improvements like the one he was vetoing. Some two years earlier, however, he cited goods like "domestic wealth," "the public defense," and "national prosperity and independence" to justify a *protective* tariff, more than a mere revenue tariff that all sides would have agreed was proper. And he ended the same address with a call on Congress to consider

> the establishment of a national seminary of learning within the District of Columbia . . . an institution [that] claims the patronage of Congress as a monument of their solicitude for the advancement of knowledge, without which the blessings of liberty cannot be fully enjoyed or long preserved; as a model instructive in the formation of other seminaries; as a nursery of enlightened preceptors, and as a central resort of youth and genius from every part of their country, diffusing on their return examples of those national feelings, those liberal sentiments, and those congenial manners which contribute cement to our Union and strength to the great political fabric of which that is the foundation.[48]

I leave Madison's apparent conflicts to his biographers and to those who claim to find constitutional meaning solely in the concrete intentions of historical figures, an approach to interpretation I criticize elsewhere.[49] My response to Madison's theory is to view it in its two aspects: the abstract theory, and his (seemingly contradictory) application of the abstract theory. The abstract theory makes sense to me. It manages to reconcile two ideas that can conflict: Congress's powers granted for the sake of national ends and Congress's powers as enumerated powers. It limits national power without suggesting

---

[46] See Pritchett, *The American Constitution*, 246–47. The quoted passage is from Madison's "Report on the Virginia Resolutions," 1799–1800, reprinted in Marvin Meyers, ed., *The Mind of the Founder: Sources of the Political Thought of James Madison* (Indianapolis: Bobbs-Merrill, 1973), 311.

[47] From Madison's veto of the Bonus Bill, March 3, 1817, reprinted in Meyers, *Mind of the Founder*, 393.

[48] Meyers, *Mind of the Founder*, 386–88.

[49] See Barber, *Constitution of Judicial Power*, chap. 4.

that the people's welfare constitutionally must sometimes yield to the reserved powers of the states. But it does this only if Congress's enumerated powers both point to *and* authorize the pursuit of that which best justifies them, that which makes normative sense of the preambulatory people's granting them in the first place: a comprehensive set of goods defined independently of the operations of the government established to pursue them. These goods include the general welfare, a general idea to which the Constitution's rights and structures impart a bourgeois liberal conception, as opposed currently to conceptions favored by the Religious Right and other antiliberals. Madison's abstract understanding of the general welfare clause makes sense; his concrete application does not. I see no way to justify granting any government coercive power over life, liberty, and property just for the pleasure of watching federal employees coin money or federal bureaucrats police the terms of interstate trade. As Madison indicates with clarity and passion in *Federalist* No. 45, these activities make sense only if they collectively envision goods like the material well-being of the population, and granting these powers to the national government on terms of the supremacy clause makes sense only if the population's material well-being outweighs goods associated with the so-called reserved powers of the states.

Madison's abstract understanding of the general welfare clause would authorize spending for any project, from protecting domestic industries to a national university, deemed conducive to a bourgeois liberal conception of the nation's material well-being. There is no political argument that can make sense of Madison's admitting that internal improvements were conducive to a "general prosperity," that the enumerated powers did envision a general prosperity, yet that Congress could not spend for internal improvements. Leonard Sorenson attributes Madison's position to his respect for opposition to internal improvements among some of the Constitution's drafters in Philadelphia and some of its ratifiers in the state ratifying conventions.[50] But Sorenson admits that the constitutional text omits any such restrictions on the spending power, and because I have argued (without successful refutation, in my view) that no argument can save Sorenson's kind of concrete originalism, especially in the teeth of reasonable textual possibilities linked to acknowledged national need (Madison repeatedly acknowledged the nation's need for federally funded internal improvements), I see no argument for Madison's position on internal improvements. I can therefore reasonably distinguish Madison's the-

---

[50] Sorenson, *Madison on the "General Welfare,"* 84.

ory, abstractly understood, from (some of) its applications, accepting the theory while rejecting applications inconsistent with the theory.

My assessment of Hamilton's theory is the converse of my view of Madison's theory. I accept the way Hamilton applied his theory without accepting his abstract formulation of it. Hamilton apparently saw "the general Welfare" for which spending was authorized as something left entirely for Congress to define, without reference to the enumerated powers. By this understanding, had it not been for the First Amendment and the Civil War amendments, Congress could have decided to fund religious establishments and antimiscegenation programs in the states on theories of well-being connected to such policies.[51] Given the Supreme Court's acceptance of Hamilton's abstract theory, possibilities of this antiliberal nature remain open today. We can see this in the current interest of the American Right in vouchers for children attending parochial schools of whatever stripe, federal funding for faith-based social programs, and the present denial of federal sex-education funds for programs that inform nonabstaining teens about condoms and other means of preventing pregnancy and disease. These possibilities would have been less likely had Congress conceived the general welfare in terms of Article I, section 8, and the enforcement provisions of the Civil War amendments. As for Hamilton's *application* of his theory, he spoke of broadly economic matters like federal spending for internal improvements and "whatever concerns the general interests of learning, of agriculture, of manufacturers, and of commerce."[52] Hamilton's theory in application thus seems close to Madison's theory in abstract formulation, and the Constitution supports either.

WELFARE AND THE COURTS

This book has concentrated on welfare and the Constitution, not welfare and the courts. The Constitution is instrumental to ends that include the general welfare regardless of what role courts might play in pursuing constitutional ends. Concern for the people's well-being shifts our attention from courts and constitutional constraints to legislative power and the public's support for constitutional aspirations.

---

[51] For an early warning against similar possibilities, see second essay of "Amphictyon," in Gerald Gunther, ed., *John Marshall's Defense of McCulloch v. Maryland* (Stanford, Calif.: Stanford University Press, 1969), 75.

[52] The quoted passage is from Hamilton's "Report on Manufacturers"; see Meyers, *Mind of the Founder*, 310.

But this does not mean no role for courts. I conclude with a sketch of how the instrumental principles elaborated in this book should orient courts in the different kinds of questions they decide.

In cases of state-federal conflict, courts should favor Congress when they perceive Congress pursuing a reasonable view of constitutional ends. This preference for Congress honors the supremacy clause and follows from the status of constitutional ends as real goods, not mere conventional goods to be defined however local majorities might wish. Ordinary moral experience and the Constitution's exclusion of some comprehensive moral commitments assume one right answer to what constitutes the general welfare. In a "pluralist" system this would be one fundamental answer overarching a plurality of derivative or compatible answers. Contrary to Justice Holmes and the value-neutral variety of pluralism he helped to found,[53] constitutional logic cannot admit fundamentally different conceptions of well-being. This favors national over state power and, as we have seen, either Hamilton's application of, or Madison's abstract reading of, the general welfare clause. On the other hand, the normative gap between opinion and truth favors a diversity of views in dialectical relationship, and that suggests room for local experiments (with "welfare reform," for example) that remain answerable to national standards and authorities.

Courts should decide against Congress when Congress acts for antiliberal ends. Antiliberal enactments exceed Congress's powers for the reasons I have stressed in this book: Congress's powers make sense only in light of liberal ends; constitutional rights and the social preconditions of constitutional institutions presuppose liberal ends; liberal ends reflect an independently attractive conception of the people's welfare; and antiliberal ends fail standards of public reasonableness that seem impossible to live without by choice. Unconstitutional congressional acts usually offend the rights of individuals under the establishment clause or the equal protection component of the Fifth Amendment. Courts should also invalidate congressional spending for other than authorized national ends, like vouchers that parents can redeem at racist schools or at schools that prepare young people for lives of submission to religious authority.[54] State support for antiliberal education would usually offend the establishment clause or the equal protection clause and undermine the secular reasonableness on which liberal constitutionalism depends. Congress can use the spending power or even the guarantee clause of Article IV to discourage these establishments.

[53] See Sandel, *Democracy's Discontent*, 43–47.

[54] See *Louisiana Financial Assistance Commission v. Poindexter*, 389 U.S. 571 (1968), voiding state tuition grants to students attending segregated schools.

The Supreme Court announced a general test for school-voucher plans when it recently approved a program in which as many as 96 percent of the participating children in Cleveland, Ohio, had enrolled in religious schools. A five-to-four majority in *Zelman v. Simmons-Harris* (2002) held that as long as the state had a secular reason (like helping poor children escape failing public schools) and the vouchers were distributed "neutrally" with regard to religion, enrollment patterns resulting from the "true private choice" of parents were of no constitutional relevance—apparently regardless of long-term educational and political consequences.[55] The Court thus approved a program that enables parents to send their children to a school whose message is that "'Christ is the basis of all learning.'" This school promises parents, "'All subjects will be taught from the Biblical perspective that all truth is God's truth.'"[56]

Zelman is confused about both the cultural conditions of constitutional democracy and the welfare of children. By requiring the state to have a secular purpose, the Court affirms the constitutional value of public reasonableness. This part of the Court's opinion belongs with a view of well-being as thinking for yourself in communities of others capable of the same. But *Zelman* would also permit the state to subvert the regime of public reasonableness through the agency of "true private choice." Acting through "true private choice" without regard for the consequences, the state could subsidize children being programmed not to think for themselves. The secular-purpose part of *Zelma*'s rule fits a regime committed to the pursuit of real goods through the dialectical representations of apparent goods by fallible beings. The "true private choice" part of *Zelman*'s rule can dispense with apparent goods and the authority of fallible beings. It opens the way to a regime where nonknowers justly submit to the power of the one who unerringly knows the good—*power* because only power can close the gap between knowledge and mere belief, the power of *one personage or group* because contending beliefs presuppose one right answer, and *just* submission to that power because all want the good that only one is sufficiently powerful to determine. In this regime the might that determines goodness makes might right. The Constitution's regime is different; here might is right only when serving goods it can neither make nor fully comprehend.

Zelman mistakenly confounds *true choice* with choice *truly private*. We have seen that choice implies reason, that choice is evident only where

[55] *Zelman v. Simmons-Harris*, 153 L.Ed. 604 (2002).

[56] Justice David Souter, dissenting at ibid., 639, and quoting from the *Westside Baptist Christian School Parent-Student Handbook*, 7.

reason is plausibly imputed, and plausible imputation involves share-able experiences and goods or apparent goods. That is why it would be hard to say that Abraham *truly chooses* to kill his innocent son. A *truly private* choice cannot be perceived as a choice. The question in the voucher controversy therefore is not whether choice is truly private, but whether parents can truly choose to program their children to live without thinking for themselves as a best they can about the most im-portant things. One can doubt that even the most religious of them could truly want their children so totally immersed in (some version of) biblical truth that they lose the ability to confirm that truth through the only process for confirming (as opposed to passively receiving) truth—namely, a good-faith consideration of evidence on the other side. It is hard to believe that, professions aside, anyone could truly choose such a life for himself, for choice implies reason, and it is hard to see how one can have a reason to live without reason. And if one can choose for one's children what one cannot truly choose for oneself, why respect the parent's choice for the children? If there is an answer to this question in particular circumstances, it centers on what is good for the children, not on the sanctity of parental choice. No one will dispute this conclusion because everyone recognizes, and the criminal law attests, that some parental choices are beneath toleration, not to mention respect.

Since no value inheres in what is truly private, what is good for the children would seem to be what an informed and publicly responsible person would confirm as good for them. The best that such a person could say in *Zelman*'s defense is (1) that experience has shown the peo-ple's well-being better served by an early education that reflects reli-gious beliefs, and (2) that the Constitution's commitment to secular reasonableness should be adjusted accordingly. But since it would take a secular argument to confirm both prongs of this position, the good served would be a secular good. We might have evidence, for example, that religiously trained youth are more likely to abstain from sex, avoid drugs, work hard in school, and become responsible parents and pro-ductive workers. Such an argument would implicitly subordinate uniquely religious goods (saving one's soul, praising God) to secular ends. Because only domesticated religions belong in this picture, the state would have to discriminate against undomesticated religions.

The Ohio program at issue in *Zelman* in fact does discriminate against some undomesticated religions. It does so by restricting eligi-bility to schools that do not promote unlawful conduct or discriminate against any religion, race, or ethnic group[57]. But the Ohio law stops

---

[57] As reported at 153 L.Ed. 612, 624–25.

short of excluding all schools that oppose the culture of secular reasonableness for which the state itself still speaks. When Ohio discriminates
against religious schools that discriminate against other religions, it
implies either that there is no religious truth or that there is no religious
truth whose vindication is worth more than peace among different
(some true, some false) religions. When it discriminates against schools
that promote unlawful conduct, it tells today's true believer that acting
as God wills can never be as important as the goods sought by the law,
goods that presently include unobstructed access to abortion clinics.
True believers can accept none of these propositions, of course. And
true believers of several stripes are working hard for the power to
change the culture that these propositions represent. *Zelman* errs in denying the constitutional relevance of these facts; even a negative constitution has cultural prerequisites.

As for rights generally, from an ends-oriented view their exercise
must be instrumental to, or at least not destructive of, constitutional
ends, and specific rights should be conceived accordingly. This view
need not imply weak rights; it can even approximate a rights absolut-
ism. The First Amendment's freedom of speech is paradigmatic here:
honoring this freedom protects criticism that the gap between truth
and opinion makes essential to forming judgments about the soundness of public policy. Speech and attendant rights of electoral review
thus appear integral to the pursuit of constitutional ends—without
them one cannot know whether the government is pursuing defensible
versions of constitutional ends. Abridging public-spirited and responsible speech for the sake of constitutional ends conceived as real goods
is thus a self-defeating act. Events may drive the government to such
acts, but the acts can never be constitutional, and governments that
would act constitutionally will pursue conditions in which they *can* act
constitutionally. This, in the abstract, is the moral of Lincoln's presidency.[58] Governments serious about negative liberties will be positive
governments.

The close alliance between deliberative democracy and ends like autonomy and "government by reflection and choice" makes the material
preconditions of deliberative democracy relevant to any suitable view
of the general welfare. Sunstein lists among conditions of deliberative
democracy "freedom from desperate conditions," freedom from "caste
systems," and "rough equality of opportunity."[59] He links these conditions to the New Deal's insistence that the Constitution, applied to
modern conditions, promises minimal "rights to food, shelter, clothing,

[58] See Barber, *On What the Constitution Means*, 140–42, 147–54, 187–96.
[59] Sunstein, *Partial Constitution*, 138–40.

medical care, education, and assistance in . . . old age or poor health" (59–60, 139). Though he joins Roosevelt in looking more to the elected branches than to the judiciary, Sunstein views these positive freedoms as "constitutional obligations" of Congress and the president (139–40). The Constitution's instrumental nature and the role of positive government in honoring strong rights and maintaining the preconditions of deliberative democracy display the Constitution as envisioning a nation whose citizens have both the intellectual, moral, and material wherewithal to criticize the government's versions of constitutional ends, and the motivation to do so that comes with a positive role in the economy and a respected voice in public affairs. A population whose members enjoy a set of political rights and realistic expectations of actual social and economic success is thus integral to the pursuit of constitutional ends.

But the instrumental Constitution can hardly treat all conceptions of admitted rights as integral to its ends. We have seen the Constitution opposed to conceptions of religious exercise that would deny freedoms from racial and sexual discrimination in education, the workplace, and community affairs.[60] Because the theory defended in this book conceives well-being largely in terms of capacities for what Lincoln called "laudable pursuits," constitutional government can condition some benefits on waiver of the freedom to decline work, if that could be done without harming the children of persons who exercise that freedom, along with people who cannot work or cannot find work. More generally, the instrumental constitution seems compatible with what Neil Gilbert has called a shift in welfare philosophy from one that views people "not as passive recipients of public benefits and care but as individuals capable of looking after themselves with occasional assistance from the government."[61] If constitutional government can spend to promote "those national feelings, those liberal sentiments, and those congenial manners which contribute cement to our Union and strength to the great political fabric of which that is the foundation," as Madison once said it could, then government can spend to promote the work ethic on which the general welfare depends.

If they want to, and some may not, instrumental constitutionalists can easily reject Richard Epstein's use of the just-compensation clause of the Fifth Amendment as a bar to government's pursuit of retirement security for the elderly, the ability of children to escape the poverty of

---

[60] See Eisgruber and Sager, "Why the Religious Freedom Restoration Act is Unconstitutional," 445–52.

[61] Neil Gilbert, *Welfare Justice: Restoring Social Equity* (New Haven, Conn.: Yale University Press, 1995), xii, 63–67, 151–54.

their parents, and other aims of the "welfare state."[62] The just-compensation clause, now applicable to all levels of government in America, bars taking of private property for a public use without just compensation. The clause has traditionally protected owners of property, tangible and intangible, from loss of title or possession, taken by government for what it declares to be a public use. Privately held land taken to build a municipal airport would be an obvious example, but the courts have also declared that if regulations of property "go too far" in specific ways, like physical occupation and denials of productive use, a "taking" has occurred for which government must compensate. Epstein contends that policies typical of the "welfare state" amount to unconstitutional takings. Taxing the rich to help the poor, he says, is (1) a taking of property (albeit a "partial taking" from many anonymous taxpayers) that (2) transfers wealth by compulsion from one class of persons to another while serving no genuine public purpose, no matter the legislature's intent, and that (3) usually fails to compensate the rich for their losses. Thus conceived, the just-compensation clause renders unconstitutional most of the social safety net since the New Deal (57–62, 93–96, 106–7, 161–69, 195–210, 281, 314–18, 324).

Epstein claims to derive his position from Locke (11–18). But Epstein and Locke disagree in important particulars. Epstein rejects Locke's restrictions on how much one person can rightfully acquire in a state of nature (11–12), and, as Thomas Grey has observed, Epstein ignores Locke's belief that the state has special obligations to the poor.[63] Epstein also ignores statesmen in the Lockean tradition like Madison and Lincoln. Madison saw the state obligated to protect not wealth so much as the faculty (of rich and poor alike) to acquire wealth, and Lincoln saw the state chiefly obligated to develop those faculties. Epstein reads Locke the way he does not from a disciple's desire to make the master's peripheral statements consistent with his core teaching but from a belief that his correction of Locke serves an overriding good. Thus, in rejecting Locke's view that, in a state of nature, first possessors of things are obligated to leave "enough, and as good . . . in common for others," Epstein says Locke was wrong to ignore the gains to everyone in honoring the first possessor's right to unlimited acquisition. "What is lost to late-comers from the world of acquisition," says Epstein, "is provided for in the world of trade and commerce for the benefit of those who did not acquire anything from the original commons."[64]

[62] See Epstein, *Takings*, 93–100, 306–8, 314–24.

[63] Thomas Grey, "The Malthusian Constitution," *University of Miami Law Review* 41 (1986): 46.

[64] Epstein, *Takings*, 11, citing Locke, *Second Treatise*, par. 27.

And in a later account of what motivates his view of the Constitution, Epstein says that "the society which adheres to the demands of the eminent domain clause will find itself better able to obtain prosperity for all its members than one which deviates from that principle."[65]

These statements mark a welfarist strain in Epstein's thinking that runs counter to the negative constitutionalism he expresses elsewhere, especially where he rejects seeking the meaning of a constitutional provision in its intended or putative purpose, where he construes the separation of powers and the representative system as restraints on government, and where he finds the "ends of government" identified by the Bill of Rights instead of the Preamble.[66] His ostensibly negative constitutionalism notwithstanding, Epstein seems a welfare constitutionalist. He evidently has his own conception of well-being, elements of which are wealth and state-guaranteed security for wealth, and he identifies these and other goods as ends that government is obligated to pursue (112). A more self-conscious welfarist would of course contain and thereby modify the negative aspects of Epstein's constitutionalism within an overarching positive view that emphasizes constitutional powers and preambulatory ends—all conceived in the public-spirited voice of the Constitution and political speech generally. This public-spirited voice is Epstein's own voice as a writer and teacher. But it is not the egoistic voice of his subject: the rational maximizer of economic theory. We have seen that within the public-spirited view, rights mark aspects of, or the conditions for, the reasonable and publicly responsible pursuit of constitutional ends. The personal autonomy that depends partly on private property would thus be both a constituent of, and a condition for, the reasonable pursuit of national defense, domestic tranquility, and other ends, including the general welfare—all understood as real goods about whose content and means individual conceptions can always be wrong.

From this basic view of rights, the just-compensation clause would have no effect on taxes designed reasonably and in good faith to secure the ends of government. Epstein does not really disagree with this general proposition. In his discussion of the police power he says that "peace and good order are the central functions of government," and by peace and good order he means, as did Locke, whom he cites, "security against possible aggression" by third parties (107–8, citing Locke, *Second Treatise*, par. 136). Epstein exempts taxes for police-power purposes from his rule that taxes are takings that are not compensated

---

[65] Richard A. Epstein, "An Outline of *Takings*," *University of Miami Law Review* 41 (1986): 3.

[66] Epstein, *Takings*, 17–18, 25–26.

for by the goods they make possible (15–16). But Epstein gives the police power a very narrow scope. He says that the "sole function of the police power is to protect individual liberty and property against force and fraud" (112). He rejects the broader view of government in the tradition that stretches from Locke to Madison, Hamilton, and Lincoln, and that justifies taxation for purported public purposes that include an educated and upwardly mobile population, the diffusion of "liberal sentiments," and the protection of domestic manufacturers. He even rejects the view of the Supreme Court in *Lochner v. New York* (1905), which saw the police power as power to pursue "the safety, health, morals, and the general welfare of the public."[67] Language this broad suggests "an unrestricted grant of state power to act in the public interest." Such power, Epstein feels, would "overwhelm the [just-compensation] clause," which, on his reading, protects the property of individuals from all restraint except those restraints (like laws against theft) that protect or increase the property of taxpayers.[68]

Epstein would admit some tax-supported help for the poor, but only when poor support "spared [the rich] the violence that would overcome them if the poor were shut out from . . . social gains." On these occasions, the rich would have to feel that "[t]he peace obtained is worth more than the money paid to obtain it." These occasions of "a clear and present danger of social unrest" from the poor would be rare, says Epstein, "where the opportunities for individual advancement were left open" and where the poor believed that "individual initiative promises relatively higher returns" than violence (316). This may be no modest concession on Epstein's part. It could suggest that the tax losses of the rich *are* compensated for if spent to achieve and maintain a broad perception of meaningful "opportunities for individual advancement." Epstein might thus allow spending to promote economic growth, remove artificial barriers to laudable pursuits, and cultivate the intellectual and psychological competences that constitute real "opportunities for individual advancement"—as did welfarists like Madison, Hamilton, Lincoln, Roosevelt, and Johnson, all without any worries of offending the just-compensation clause. But Epstein tries to close this opening for his critics. He speaks not of government actively working to facilitate and maintain opportunities for individual advancement, but rather of government's passively leaving such opportunities open, in apparent confidence that the first possessors will do the same with sufficient regularity to compensate latecomers whose original opportunities were taken by the first possessors. His summary

[67] 198 U.S. 45, 53 (1905).
[68] Epstein, *Takings*, 109.

strategy for a regime of individual opportunity is simply "limited government," and as an example of the barriers he has in mind, he mentions the minimum wage (316). Government can legitimately tax,
spend and regulate to protect the property of the rich from force and
fraud, but apparently not, or not as readily, to protect that same property from the social conditions and perceptions of illegitimacy that
threaten it.

As it turns out, the difference between Epstein and other welfare
constitutionalists has less to do with the just-compensation clause and
the relationship between welfare and the Constitution than with such
issues as what constitutes the general welfare and how best to pursue
it. Welfare constitutionalists not only do debate these things among
themselves; they must, as we have seen. For Epstein as for other welfare constitutionalists, the just-compensation clause is no burden on
the taxing power when government is doing the right thing. The clause
just serves to clarify for Epstein what the right thing is; it serves the
same function as the First and Fourteenth Amendments do in my hypothesis. For Epstein as for other welfare constitutionalists, moreover,
the right thing serves the good thing, or what is rightfully seen as the
good thing. We recall here his statement that honoring the just-compensation clause as he sees it would make society "better able to obtain
prosperity for all its members."

As for judicially enforced positive rights under the Fourteenth
Amendment, the Supreme Court has found many such rights, including access to the courts for businesses involved in labor disputes, freedom from state residency requirements for persons otherwise eligible
for public assistance, the right to attend racially nondiscriminatory
public schools, and appointed legal counsel for indigent criminal de-
fendants.[69] The Court, however, has held that the government is not
obligated to provide the poor with noncustodial rights to education,
public assistance, decent housing, or medical care.[70] And we have seen
the *DeShaney* Court's avoiding the slippery slope to judicially enforced
welfare rights by denying a state's obligation to protect a child from
predictable violence. Whether the instrumental Constitution argues
against all or any of these decisions depends partly on what theory of
individual and social well-being the Constitution is thought to embody
and partly on what courts can achieve within conventions that separate judicial from nonjudicial action. These conventions are hardly so

---

[69] *Truax v. Corrigan*, 257 U.S. 312 (1921); *Shapiro v. Thompson*, 394 U.S. 618 (1969); *Brown
v. Board of Education*, 347 U.S. 483 (1954); *Gideon v. Wainwright*, 372 U.S. 335 (1963).

[70] *San Antonio v. Rodriguez*, 411 U.S. 1 (1972); *Dandridge v. Williams*, 397 U.S. 471 (1970);
Lindsey v. Normet, 405 U.S. 56 (1972); *Harris v. McRae*, 448 U.S. 297 (1980).

rigid that they preclude results different from those the Court reached in the school funding and police protection cases. We have seen that a negative libertarian like Currie never questions the appropriateness of referring to the German Constitutional Court as a *court*, notwithstanding that court's findings of positive rights to education and fetal life under the Basic Law. And federal judges in America might well look closer than Judge Bork might wish at his own suggestion that they can exhort policy makers and the public in the Constitution's name.[71]

But an instrumental constitutionalist cannot avoid concluding either that courts have a limited role in facilitating individual and social welfare or that the greater role belongs to the legislature and the taxpaying electorate. The Constitution obligates the government to facilitate the real well-being of all its people, and there is no compelling reason to conclude that there is no approximate truth about the elements of well-being. Nor must we deny that a plausible interpretation of constitutional text and history can accommodate an approximation of that truth. But the complex, contingent, and unpredictable character of policies for facilitating any conception of well-being, together with the time-sensitive balance of needs involved in concrete funding decisions—and the ultimate need for public support—place most of the responsibility on legislators and their voting constituents.[72]

This is bad news for those who see easy application to concrete cases or political practice as a requirement for propositions of constitutional theory. If government is obligated to protect and develop the natural faculties of poor children, say, and if technological change and the economic leverage of the propertied combine to leave those faculties unprotected unless government alters the status quo, good government will want to do what it can. The consolation of its propertied constituents—their "compensation," if you will—must in the end be found in an enlarged conception of who they are. Constitutional theory thus points as much to attitudes as to rules; this may explain the civic republicanism of positive constitutionalists like Michelman, Sunstein, and Sandel.[73]

The need for what Sandel calls a new public philosophy raises sobering questions about the Constitution's adequacy to its ends. For there is little doubt that a strong element of elite and popular attitudes in America either subordinates public to private purposes or understands

[71] See Barber, *On What the Constitution Means*, 202–4.

[72] Sager, "Justice in Plain Clothes," 420–25; Sunstein, *Partial Constitution*, 139, 145–49; Michelman, "Welfare Rights in a Constitutional Democracy," 684–85; see also Rosenberg, *The Hollow Hope*, 10–36.

[73] See Frank Michelman, "Law's Republic," *Yale Law Journal* 97 (1983): 1493; Sunstein, *Partial Constitution*, 133–41; Sandel, *Democracy's Discontent*, 200–203, 280, 346.

the former as derivative of the latter. There is also little doubt that the Constitution itself is partly responsible for this situation.[74] Benjamin Barber joins Walter Berns and others in attributing this attitude to the constitutional decisions of the founding. But unlike Berns, Barber emphasizes the founding's corrosive effects on citizenship and public purposes. Barber sees indifference to public purposes as stemming from the framers' strategy for engineering cooperation through the private incentives of a commercial society. Separated from public purposes, citizenship is conceived less in terms of opportunities for the exercise of virtue and more in terms of legal rights to represent one's demands against others.[75]

Separation from public purposes seems also to have changed the related notions of reason and responsibility from public-spirited reasonableness to personal economic calculation and the skills of helping one's self—from Publius's notions of reason and responsibility to those of Murray, Winter, Bork, and Epstein. The propertied "help themselves" in two senses, though many admit only to one, and the poor who feel trapped in poverty may see no reason not to help themselves in the blameworthy sense. As Hobbesian attitudes recrudesce, the culture of self-serving incentives becomes increasingly indifferent to the chronically poor, feeding doubts about the Constitution's competence to its ends. Since well-being has much to do with competence toward one's ends, indifference to the poor takes something away from the well-being not only of the poor but also of those persons (if any) who see themselves as part of the Constitution's preambulatory "We." They now have reason to doubt their capacity as individuals to constitute a preambulatory "We." This brings doubts about their capacity as individuals not only to establish and maintain constitutions but also to pursue real goods—real goods as opposed to apparent goods, goods imposed by "accident and force." For if real goods exist, they are approximated through dialectical processes that presuppose things like reasonably diverse yet well-ordered communities of interlocutors whose language bespeaks a common world about which they, collectively and individually, can err. If for any reason—social-psychological, economic, metaphysical—bourgeois liberalism cannot establish or maintain such communities, one can deny the competence and therewith the well-being of bourgeois liberalism and of bourgeois liberals as such. This problem underscores the dependence of bourgeois liber-

---

[74] See Barber, Constitution of Judicial Power, 113, 235–36.

[75] Benjamin R. Barber, "The Compromised Republic: Public Purposelessness in America," in Robert Horwitz, ed., The Moral Foundations of the American Republic (Charlottesville: University Press of Virginia, 1986), 47–48.

alism on virtues and attitudes that may depend on the market but are neither associated with the market nor cultivated by it and indeed may not survive its influences—virtues such as those associated with academe, which justifies itself in terms of the disciplined and self-critical pursuit of truth,[76] and the regulatory bureaucracy, which justifies itself in terms of public-spirited competence in delivering public goods.[77] The welfare debate thus implicates broader problems of constitutional and cultural reform.

The Constitution, by its language and the object lesson of its founding, claims the fidelity of the population only in terms of the benefits it facilitates. The population must in principle be able to recognize the Constitution as an approximation of what it says it is, and that requires at least some evidence of progress toward its ends. The condition for fidelity to the Constitution is thus one and the same as the condition for its recognition as a coherent scheme. Officials who get paid to maintain the Constitution get paid to work for the conditions that can justify seeing and following the Constitution for what it claims to be, for that is essentially what it means to maintain the Constitution.[78] Judges thus have a constitutional reason to construe the Fourteenth Amendment and other constitutional provisions accordingly, where they prudently can.

Ideological conservatives in America (sometimes) detest the proposition that mere failure of the elected branches to address a social problem licenses judicial action. They see this proposition circumventing both democracy and the Constitution.[79] But constitutionalists can defend the proposition. As a means to ends like the people's welfare, the Constitution fails to the extent that the government it established seems chronically incapable of serious effort to correct the disabling conditions under which millions live. To avoid this conclusion, one might shift responsibility from the Constitution to the government and say that the government helps perpetuate conditions that mock the purposes of its establishment. But in neither of these situations is the Constitution working. Where the evidence indicates either that the Consti-

---

[76] For criticism of Stanley Fish's attempt to deflate this justification for the academy, see Sotirios A. Barber, "Stanley Fish and the Future of Pragmatism in Legal Theory," *University of Chicago Law Review* 58 (1991): 1033, 1036–43.

[77] See Herbert J. Storing, "Political Parties and the Bureaucracy," in Robert A. Goldwin, ed., *Political Parties U.S.A.* (Chicago: Rand McNally, 1965), 151–58.

[78] I elaborate this point in "A Note on Constitutional Maintenance," in Barber and George, eds., *Constitutional Politics*, 162–67.

[79] See, e.g., Winter, "Poverty, Economic Equality, and the Equal Protection Clause," 93; contrast *Bush v. Gore*, 531 U.S. 98, at 111.

tution has failed or that the government it established is chronically incapable of following it, the Constitution ceases to be effective law.

A court or any political actor that believes itself to be in either of these constitutionally ungoverned situations can look to Lincoln's presidency for examples of constitutional*ist* action without constitu*tional* warrant. Where the Constitution is no longer effective law, there can be no constitutional reason for not doing what one can do to restore or achieve the conditions for the Constitution's effectiveness.[80] That would include finding judicially enforceable welfare rights in the Fourteenth Amendment, even some beyond the framers' concrete intentions. One might begin with a right to education in a nonsectarian, integrated public school that promotes "those liberal sentiments" that Madison saw as foundational to the Union and thus to the good that *Federalist* No. 45 says the Union is instrumental to: "the real welfare of the great body of the people."

---

[80] Barber, *On What the Constitution Means*, 189–90, 201–4. For a related argument that preserves some constitutional constraints even in emergencies that call for "suspend[ing] a wide variety of individual liberties," see Finn, *Constitutions in Crisis*, 40–43.

INDEX

action-inaction distinction. *See* state inaction

Addams, Jane: and pre–New Deal attitudes toward public relief for the poor, 35; and virtues of positive constitutionalists, 85

affirmative action: as means to constitutional end, 47; and dependence of rights on public attitudes, 54

Allen, Ronald: as negative constitutionalist, 79–80; and criticism of moral realism, 79, 81, 86

Anti-Federalists: and national powers as threat to liberty, 43; and Tenth Amendment, as concession to, 127; as framers, 127

antiliberalism: as antirationalism, 62, 90, 113; as constitutionally disfavored, 75–76, 88–90, 107, 110, 122–23, 125, 128, 135; constitutional power to discourage attitudes of, 4, 53–55; and false claims of liberal neutrality, 88–90; justifying opposition to, 110–14; limited constitutional protection of, 135–36; limited toleration of, in liberal culture, 62; as not choiceworthy, 62, 141, 145; presence of, as element of constitutional power, 136; and reason, 62, 90, 110–14, 141, 145; and unconstitutional ends, 89

Aristotle: and fallibility of perceived wants, 105; and property as social institution, 50

Articles of Confederation, 88

Bandes, Susan: on arguments against welfare rights, 43; on need for theory of constitutional ends, 43

Barber, Benjamin: on public purposelessness as legacy of American founding, 153

Barry, Norman: antiwelfarist view of free market, 10; on distinguishing "welfare" from "justice" and "rights," 17–22; on implicitly objective conception of well-being, 10; as moral subjectivist, 10–11,

17, 22; on narrow conception of "welfare," 12; on "promiscuity of welfare," 16; on protecting negative rights as redistributive, 14; on social insurance as redistributive, 14n.18; on state welfare as method of controlling the poor, 27; on welfarist view of free market, 14

benefits (welfarist) model, of U.S. Constitution. *See* positive constitutionalism

Bentham, Jeremy: and view of general welfare as objective state of affairs, 10

Berlin, Isaiah: on minimal welfarist duty of government, 26; on self government as end in itself, 51

Berns, Walter: as "big government" conservative, 38, 63–64; on bourgeois ends of liberal constitutionalism, 76–77; on *The Federalist*, 38, 103; on foundations of tolerance, 76, 82; as positive constitutionalist, 63–64; on social conditions of Constitution's authority, 94

Bill of Rights: implications of, for the general welfare, 122

Black, Charles: against preference utilitarian view of general welfare, 116; as positive constitutionalist, 38

Boerne v. Flores (1997), 130n.25

Bork, Robert: on hortatory use of judicial power, 70, 152; on obligation to follow immoral regime, 94

Boy Scouts of America: antiliberalism of, 130–31, 136

Boy Scouts of America v. Dale (2000), 130–31

Brennan, William: on racial justice as constitutional end, 47; on state's duty to prevent third-party violence, 82

Brown v. Board of Education (1954), 157

Bush v. Gore (2000), 131

Calabresi, Steven: as negative constitutionalist, 44n.33

Catholicism: Americanization of, 60

Ceaser, James: on American Right's need for active government, 73n.36